Low Cholesterol Cookbook for Beginners

1800 Days of Heart-Healthy, Delicious, Tasty & Nutritious Recipes to Lower Your Cholesterol and Protect Your Heart. Includes an Easy 28-Day Meal Plan

Amanda Ray

© **Copyright 2024 - All rights reserved.**

The content contained within this book may not be reproduced, duplicated, or transmitted without direct written permission from the author or publisher.

Under no circumstances will any blame or legal responsibility be held against the publisher or author for any damages, reparations, or monetary losses due to the information contained within this book, either directly or indirectly.

Legal Notice:

This book is copyright-protected. It is only for personal use. You cannot amend, distribute, sell, use, quote, or paraphrase any part or the content within it without the consent of the author or publisher.

Disclaimer Notice:

Please note that the information contained within this document is for educational and entertainment purposes only. All efforts have been made to present accurate, up-to-date, reliable, and complete information. No warranties of any kind are declared or implied. Readers acknowledge that the author is not engaged in the rendering of legal, financial, medical, or professional advice. The content within this book has been derived from various sources. Please consult a licensed professional before attempting any techniques outlined in this book.

By reading this document, the reader agrees that under no circumstances is the author responsible for any losses, direct or indirect, that are incurred as a result of the use of the information contained within this document, including, but not limited to, errors, omissions, or inaccuracies.

Table of Content

Introduction 6

Chapter 1. About Low Cholesterol 7
The Nature of Cholesterol 7
Cholesterol and Your Health 8
The Dietary Connection 9
Lifestyle and Cholesterol 11

Chapter 2: Breakfast 13
Oatmeal with Fresh Berries and Almonds ... 13
Spinach and Mushroom Egg White Omelette 13
Avocado Toast on Whole Grain Bread 14
Greek Yogurt Parfait with Honey and Nuts 15
Banana Pancakes with Low-Fat Yogurt Topping 15
Smoothie Bowl with Chia Seeds and Kiwi 16
Whole Wheat Veggie Wraps 16
Baked Sweet Potato and Kale Hash 17
Quinoa Porridge with Cinnamon Apples 18
Low-Fat Cottage Cheese with Pineapple 18
Vegan Tofu Scramble with Tomatoes 19
Overnight Chia Seed Pudding 19
Whole Grain Blueberry Muffins 20

Chapter 3: Snacks and Appetizers 21
Carrot and Cucumber Sticks with Hummus 21
Roasted Chickpeas with Paprika 21
Baked Kale Chips 22
Almonds and Walnuts Trail Mix 22
Stuffed Bell Peppers with Quinoa 23
Edamame with Sea Salt 24
Fruit Kebabs with Yogurt Dip 24
Zucchini Fritters 24
Baked Apple Chips 25
Caprese Salad Skewers 26
Rice Cakes with Avocado Spread 26
Roasted Brussel Sprouts with Balsamic Glaze 27
Sweet Potato Wedges with Low-Fat Greek Yogurt Dip 27

Chapter 4: Poultry Dishes 29
Grilled Chicken Salad with Mixed Greens 29
Turkey Lettuce Wraps 29
Chicken and Vegetable Stir-Fry 30
Baked Chicken with Herbs and Lemon 31
Turkey Quinoa Meatballs 31

Chicken and Broccoli Alfredo (with Whole Wheat Pasta) 32
Turkey Chili with Beans 33
Baked Lemon Pepper Chicken 33
Chicken Vegetable Soup 34
Herb Roasted Turkey Breast 34
Chicken Fajitas with Whole Wheat Tortillas 35
Moroccan Spiced Chicken Skewers 36
BBQ Pulled Chicken (with Homemade Low-Sugar Sauce) 36

Chapter 5: Vegan and Vegetarian Mains 38
Stuffed Bell Peppers with Lentils 38
Vegetarian Chili 39
Tofu Stir-Fry with Mixed Vegetables 39
Vegetable Curry with Brown Rice 40
Vegan Lentil Burgers 41
Zucchini Lasagna (with Tofu Ricotta) ... 41
Stir-Fried Quinoa with Veggies 42
Eggplant Parmesan (Vegan Version) 43
Vegan Shepherd's Pie 43
Mushroom Stroganoff 44
Spaghetti Squash with Marinara Sauce 45
Roasted Cauliflower Tacos 46
Vegan Paella with Bell Peppers and Peas 46

Chapter 6: Beef Dishes 48
Grilled Flank Steak with Chimichurri 48
Beef and Broccoli Stir-Fry 48
Lean Beef Burgers with Whole Wheat Buns 49
Beef Stew with Root Vegetables 50
Beef Lettuce Wraps 50
Sirloin Steak with Grilled Vegetables 51
Beef Fajitas with Whole Wheat Tortillas 52
Beef and Mushroom Skewers 52

Slow Cooker Beef and Tomato Stew 53
Beef and Barley Soup 54
Lean Meatloaf with Oats 54
Beef and Spinach Stuffed Peppers 55
Balsamic Marinated Roast Beef 55

Chapter 7: Fish and Seafood 57
Grilled Salmon with Lemon and Dill 57
Baked Cod with Tomato and Basil 57
Shrimp Stir-Fry with Vegetables 58
Seafood Paella (with Brown Rice) 59
Tuna Salad Stuffed Avocado 59
Fish Tacos with Cabbage Slaw 60
Mussels in White Wine and Garlic Sauce 61
Baked Tilapia with Roasted Vegetables 61
Crab Cakes with Yogurt Dill Sauce 62
Clam Chowder (Lightened Version) 63
Grilled Scallops with Lemon Butter Sauce 63
Salmon Patties with Whole Wheat Breadcrumbs 64
Spicy Shrimp and Quinoa Bowl 65

Chapter 8: Salads and Side Dishes 66
Kale and Quinoa Salad with Lemon Vinaigrette 66
Roasted Beet and Goat Cheese Salad 66
Grilled Vegetable Platter 67
Couscous with Roasted Veggies 68
Sweet Corn and Black Bean Salad 68
Asparagus with Balsamic Tomatoes 69
Greek Salad with Low-Fat Feta 70
Cauliflower Rice Pilaf 70
Broccoli and Apple Salad with Walnuts 71
Roasted Carrot and Avocado Salad 72
Spinach and Strawberry Salad 72
Butternut Squash Soup 73

Green Beans Almondine..................................74

Chapter 9: Desserts 75
Baked Apples with Cinnamon 75
Low-Fat Berry Yogurt Parfait......................75
Dark Chocolate-Dipped Strawberries 76
Banana Bread with Almond Flour 76
Peach and Blueberry Crumble 77
Carrot Cake with Low-Fat Cream Cheese Frosting..78
Almond and Date Energy Balls 78
Vegan Chocolate Mousse 79
Fruit Salad with Mint and Honey 80
Oatmeal Raisin Cookies (Low Sugar) 80
Pumpkin Pie with Whole Wheat Crust 81
Grilled Pineapple with Honey Drizzle..........81
Pear and Ginger Compote 82

Chapter 10: Beverages 83
Green Tea Smoothie 83
Vegetable Juice Blend 83
Herbal Iced Tea with Lemon.......................84
Almond Milk Hot Cocoa 85
Berry and Spinach Smoothie.......................85
Tomato and Cucumber Gazpacho................86
Coconut Water and Pineapple Juice 86
Carrot and Ginger Juice 87
Beetroot and Apple Smoothie 87
Lemon and Mint Infused Water.................. 88
Pomegranate and Blueberry Spritzer.......... 88
Chamomile and Honey Tea 89
Turmeric and Ginger Latte..........................89

Chapter 11: 28-Day Meal Prep Plan 91
Week 1... 91
Week 2...92
Week 3...93
Week 4...94

Free Gift 96
Conclusion outline 97
References 98
Appendix 1: Measurement Conversion Chart 99
Appendix 2: Index Recipes 100
A..100
B..100
C..100
D... 101
E.. 101
F.. 101
G... 101
H... 101
K... 101
L.. 101
M... 101
N... 101
O... 101
P.. 101
Q...102
R...102
S..102
T..102
W...102
Y..102
Z..102

Notes..103

Introduction

Welcome to the Low Cholesterol Cookbook for Beginners – your first step towards a heart-healthy future. As a professional nutritionist and cook, I understand the challenges of making dietary changes, especially when you're just starting. This cookbook is designed to guide you through the basics of a low-cholesterol diet without sacrificing flavor or convenience.

High cholesterol is a common concern that can lead to serious health issues if not appropriately managed. The good news is that diet is one of the most effective ways to lower your cholesterol. By making simple changes to your foods, you can significantly improve your cholesterol levels and overall health.

In this cookbook, you'll find a collection of delicious recipes that are low in cholesterol and saturated fats but high in taste and nutritional value. Each recipe has been carefully crafted to be easy to follow, using readily available ingredients that support your health goals. Whether you're a seasoned cook or new to the kitchen, these recipes will empower you to create satisfying meals that help keep your cholesterol in check.

We'll also provide you with essential information on how nutrition and specific foods impact cholesterol levels so you can choose what to eat. From understanding the role of fiber and healthy fats to identifying foods to buy or avoid, this cookbook is more than just recipes – it's a comprehensive guide to healthier eating.

Remember, caring for your health is a journey, not a destination. With each meal you prepare from this cookbook, you're taking a positive step towards a healthier heart and a happier life. Let's get cooking!

Chapter 1. About Low Cholesterol

Embarking on a journey toward better health can be both exciting and daunting, but understanding the role of cholesterol and how to manage it through diet can be a game-changer. Cholesterol is a waxy substance in your blood, necessary for building cells and producing certain hormones. However, too much cholesterol can increase the risk of heart disease and stroke.

The goal of a low-cholesterol diet is to reduce the intake of saturated fats and trans fats, which are known to increase LDL cholesterol levels. Instead, the focus is on consuming foods rich in fiber and healthy fats, which can help lower LDL levels and raise high-density lipoprotein (HDL).

As a beginner, you might wonder what foods to embrace and which to avoid. The key is balance and moderation. Foods high in soluble fiber, such as oats, fruits, beans, and vegetables, can help reduce cholesterol absorption. Lean proteins like chicken, fish, and legumes are excellent choices for a low-cholesterol diet. Additionally, incorporating healthy fats from sources like avocados, nuts, and olive oil can be beneficial.

In this chapter, we'll delve into what makes a diet heart-healthy. We'll discuss the importance of reading food labels, understanding the different types of fats, and how to make smarter choices when dining out. You'll learn how to replace saturated fats with unsaturated fats in your cooking and increase your fiber-rich foods intake.

Remember, small changes can lead to big results. By gradually incorporating these dietary adjustments, you'll not only lower your cholesterol but also improve your overall health. It's not about depriving yourself but finding delicious, healthier alternatives that satisfy your taste buds and your body's needs.

As you turn the pages of this cookbook, you'll discover that a low-cholesterol diet can be diverse, flavorful, and full of the foods you love. With each recipe, you'll take a step towards a healthier heart and a more vibrant life. So let's begin this journey with optimism and a spoonful of knowledge, as we explore the world of low-cholesterol cooking together.

The Nature of Cholesterol

What is cholesterol and what are its different types?

As we embark on this culinary journey to better health, let's start with the basics: What exactly is cholesterol? In simple terms, cholesterol is a waxy, fat-like substance that's found in all the cells of your body. It's vital to create cell membranes, certain hormones, and vitamin D. Your body needs cholesterol to function properly, but too much of it can be a problem.

Cholesterol doesn't dissolve in water, so it can't travel through your blood on its own. It gets around your body by attaching to proteins. These cholesterol-protein packages are called lipoproteins. There are different types of lipoproteins, but the two most important ones are low-density lipoprotein (LDL) and high-density lipoprotein (HDL).

LDL is often referred to as «bad» cholesterol. When you have too much LDL in your blood, it can build up on the walls of your arteries. This buildup is known as plaque. Over time, plaque can narrow your arteries and increase your risk for heart disease and stroke. That's why our goal in this cookbook is to help you lower your LDL levels.

HDL, on the other hand, is known as «good» cholesterol. It aids in removing cholesterol in different forms from your blood. Reduced risk of heart disease is linked to higher levels of HDL cholesterol.

Your body makes all the cholesterol it needs, but you also get it from food. Cholesterol is found only in animal products, such as meat, dairy, and eggs. Plant-based foods do not contain cholesterol.

Now, you might wonder, «How can I manage my cholesterol levels through diet?» The key is to focus on foods that can help lower LDL cholesterol and increase HDL cholesterol. This includes eating more fruits, vegetables, whole grains, and fish while limiting saturated and trans fats found in many processed and fried foods.

Understanding cholesterol is the first step in taking control of your health. Throughout this cookbook, we'll explore how to cook and eat to support healthy cholesterol levels and a healthy heart. So, let's keep this knowledge in mind as we move forward with delicious, heart-friendly recipes that you and your family will love.

Cholesterol and Your Health

Cholesterol's Effects

As we continue our journey through the Low Cholesterol Cookbook for Beginners, it's crucial to understand how cholesterol affects your health. While cholesterol is essential for various bodily functions, it's a delicate balance. Too much of it, especially the wrong kind, can lead to serious health issues.

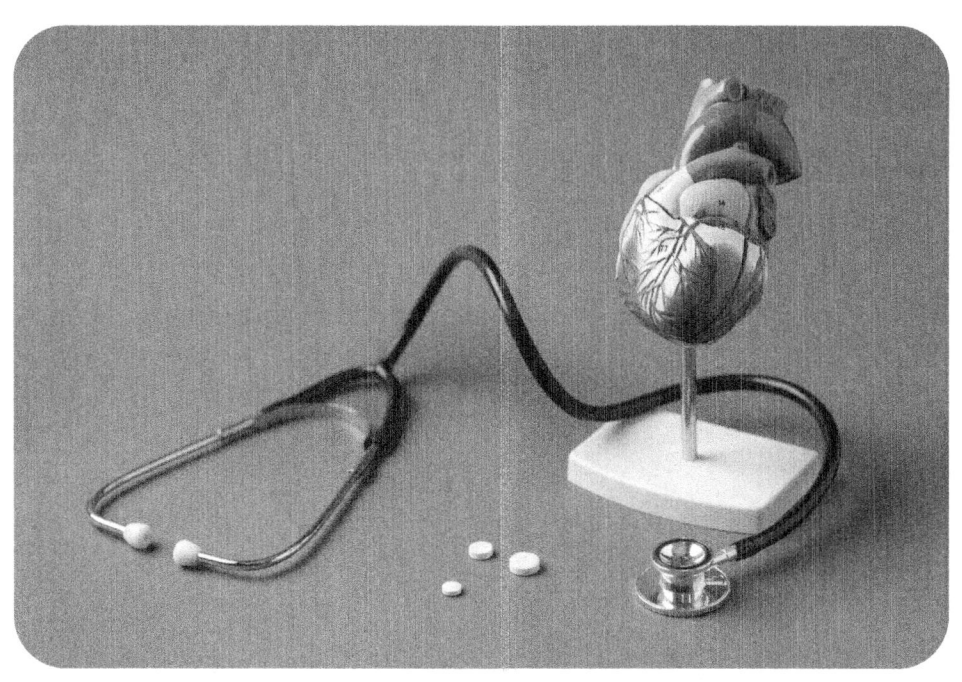

Cholesterol is involved in producing cell membranes, certain hormones, and vitamin D. However when levels of low-density lipoprotein (LDL) cholesterol are high, it can lead to the buildup of plaque in artery walls, known as atherosclerosis. This buildup can cause arteries to narrow and harden, which increases the risk of cardiovascular diseases, such as heart attacks and strokes.

High-density lipoprotein (HDL) cholesterol, on the other hand, has a protective effect on your health. It helps remove LDL cholesterol from the arteries, transporting it to the liver to be processed and eliminated from the body. Maintaining high levels of HDL cholesterol is beneficial and can reduce the risk of heart disease.

It's not just about the numbers, though. The ratio of LDL to HDL cholesterol is also important. A higher ratio means a higher risk of heart disease, while a lower ratio means a lower risk. That's why in this cookbook, we focus on foods and recipes that help improve this ratio, favoring heart health.

You may be surprised to learn that not all cholesterol comes from the food we eat. In fact, your body, specifically your liver, produces cholesterol on its own. Dietary cholesterol, which comes from animal-based foods, has a more minor impact on your blood cholesterol levels than the amount of saturated and trans fats you eat.

This doesn't mean that dietary choices aren't important. Foods rich in saturated and trans fats can significantly increase LDL cholesterol levels. Therefore, making mindful choices about what you eat is crucial. By following the recipes and tips in this cookbook, you can create meals that are not only delicious but also beneficial for maintaining healthy cholesterol levels.

In summary, while cholesterol is necessary for health, too much of the wrong kind can lead to cardiovascular diseases. By understanding cholesterol's effects and making informed dietary choices, you can take control of your health and reduce your risk of heart disease.

As we move forward, remember that your diet is a powerful tool for managing cholesterol and protecting your heart. Let's use this knowledge to cook meals that nourish our bodies and support our well-being.

Recognizing High Cholesterol

One key aspect of cholesterol and health is knowing how to recognize if you have high cholesterol. This invisible health marker can be tricky because high cholesterol doesn't usually come with clear signs or symptoms. That's why it's often called a «silent» condition, which can go undetected without proper screening.

Cholesterol levels are measured through a simple blood test called a lipid panel. This test provides information about your total cholesterol, LDL (bad) cholesterol, HDL (good) cholesterol, and triglycerides (another type of fat in your blood). High cholesterol is diagnosed when these numbers exceed healthy limits.

So, what numbers should you be looking for? Generally, for adults, a total cholesterol level below 200 milligrams per deciliter (mg/dL) is considered desirable. LDL cholesterol should be less than 100 mg/dL, and HDL cholesterol should be 60 mg/dL or higher. Triglycerides should ideally be under 150 mg/dL.

Recognizing high cholesterol through numbers is one thing, but understanding what contributes to it is another. Several factors can raise your cholesterol levels, including an unhealthy diet, lack of physical activity, smoking, obesity, and genetics. Eating foods high in saturated and trans fats, such as fatty cuts of meat, full-fat dairy products, and fried or processed foods, can increase your LDL cholesterol.

Being aware of these factors is crucial because managing your cholesterol often starts with lifestyle changes. In this cookbook, we'll provide you with delicious recipes that are low in the foods that contribute to high cholesterol and rich in those that can help lower it.

Remember, recognizing high cholesterol isn't just about the numbers from your latest blood test. It's also about being mindful of your lifestyle and the choices you make every day. By understanding the role cholesterol plays in your health and how to identify high cholesterol, you can take proactive steps towards a heart-healthy life.

As we continue to explore the connection between diet and cholesterol, we'll discover that food is not just a source of pleasure but also a powerful medicine. Let's make every meal an opportunity to nourish our bodies and safeguard our health.

The Dietary Connection

Diet's Role in Cholesterol Control

Starting the journey to manage your cholesterol can seem daunting, but it's important to recognize the powerful role your diet plays in this process. Your daily food choices directly influence your cholesterol levels, and therefore, your risk of heart disease. In this chapter, we'll delve into how diet affects cholesterol and how you can harness this knowledge to take control of your health.

Firstly, it's crucial to understand that not all fats are created equal. Saturated and trans fats, often found in processed foods, baked goods, and certain cuts of meat, can raise your LDL («bad») cholesterol levels. Conversely, unsaturated fats, such as those in olive oil, avocados, and nuts, can have a beneficial effect on your cholesterol profile by lowering LDL and potentially raising HDL («good») cholesterol.

Fruits, vegetables, whole grains, and legumes are high in fiber, which is important for lowering cholesterol. Soluble fiber, in particular, can reduce the absorption of cholesterol into your bloodstream. Including these fiber-rich foods in your diet can help reduce overall cholesterol levels.

Another aspect of the dietary connection is the balance between dietary cholesterol and the cholesterol your body naturally produces. While your liver produces all the cholesterol you need, consuming high amounts of dietary cholesterol can tip the scales and lead to elevated blood cholesterol levels. However, the impact of dietary cholesterol on blood cholesterol is less than that of saturated and trans fats.

Incorporating heart-healthy foods into your diet is not just about subtracting the bad; it's also about adding the good. Foods rich in omega-3 fatty acids, like salmon and flaxseeds, can improve heart health by reducing triglycerides and potentially increasing HDL cholesterol. Berries and leafy greens are two examples of foods high in antioxidants that can help stop LDL cholesterol from oxidizing, which is a crucial stage in the development of atherosclerosis.

Through the recipes and guidance provided in this cookbook, you'll learn how to create delicious meals that are not only satisfying but also beneficial for your cholesterol levels. By making conscious food choices, you can influence your cholesterol in a positive way and take a proactive stance towards a healthier heart.

Remember, your diet is a central factor in cholesterol control. With each meal, you have the opportunity to make choices that support your health. Let's take use of this ability and modify our diets for a lifetime of health.

Foods to Choose and Avoid

Welcome to the heart of our Low Cholesterol Cookbook for Beginners, where we navigate the dietary choices essential for managing cholesterol. Understanding which foods to embrace and which to limit can be your strongest ally in maintaining a heart-healthy lifestyle.

Foods to Choose:

1. Fruits and Vegetables: These are your best friends in the cholesterol battle. Rich in fiber and antioxidants, they help fight inflammation and lower LDL cholesterol. Aim for a rainbow of colors to maximize nutrient intake.

2. Whole Grains: Oats, barley, and whole wheat contain soluble fiber, which reduces the absorption of cholesterol into your bloodstream. Incorporate them into your meals as a base for stews or as a hearty breakfast.

3. Lean Proteins: Opt for poultry without skin, lean cuts of meat, and plant-based proteins like beans and lentils. These choices are lower in saturated fat, making them better for your cholesterol levels.

4. Fatty Fish: Salmon, mackerel, and albacore tuna are high in omega-3 fatty acids, which can lower triglycerides and boost HDL cholesterol. Aim for two servings a week.

5. Nuts and Seeds: Almonds, walnuts, and flaxseeds are not only crunchy and satisfying but also packed with healthy fats and fiber.

Foods to Avoid:

1. Trans Fats: Often found in processed foods, margarine, and snacks, trans fats can increase LDL cholesterol and lower HDL cholesterol. Read labels carefully and avoid products with «hydrogenated oils.»

2. Saturated Fats: These are prevalent in red meat, full-fat dairy products, and coconut oil. Limiting these can help reduce LDL cholesterol. When you do consume dairy, opt for low-fat or fat-free versions.

3. Processed Meats: Sausages, bacon, and processed deli meats are high in saturated fats and sodium, which are not conducive to cholesterol health.

4. Sugary Treats: High sugar intake can lead to weight gain, which indirectly can affect cholesterol levels. Limiting foods like sodas, candies, and baked goods with added sugars is best.

5. Alcohol: Excessive alcohol intake can increase cholesterol and triglyceride levels. Moderation is key.

Remember, small changes can make a big difference. Swapping out saturated fats for healthier fats, increasing fiber intake, and choosing whole foods over processed ones are simple strategies that go a long way.

With every meal and snack, you have a choice. Use this guide to choose wisely, and enjoy the journey to better health with every delicious bite.

Lifestyle and Cholesterol

Beyond Diet

While diet plays a crucial role in managing cholesterol levels, it's not the only factor to consider. A holistic approach to cholesterol health includes various lifestyle choices that can significantly impact your overall well-being. In this chapter, we'll explore how integrating positive lifestyle habits can complement your dietary efforts and contribute to better cholesterol management.

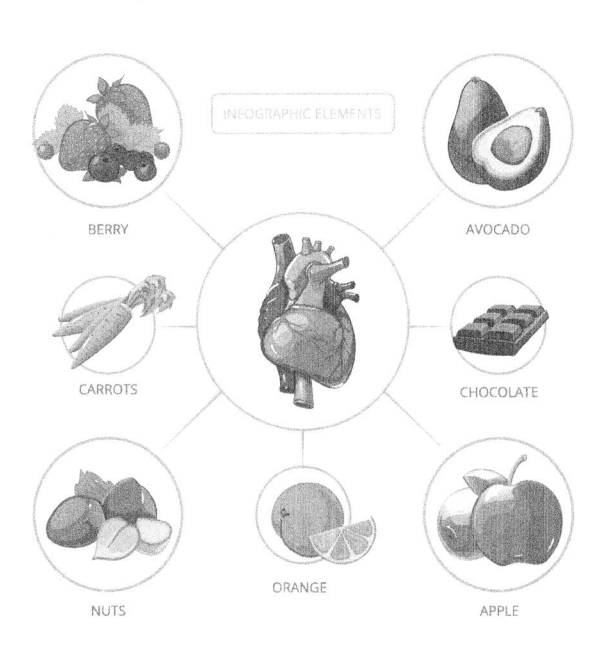

Physical Activity: Regular exercise is a cornerstone of heart health. Engaging in physical activity can help raise HDL (good) cholesterol and lower LDL (bad) cholesterol and triglycerides. You don't have to run marathons to reap the benefits; brisk walking, cycling, or swimming for 30 minutes a day can make a difference. Find an activity you enjoy, and make it a part of your routine.

Weight Management: Carrying extra weight can contribute to high cholesterol. Losing even a small percentage of body weight can help lower your cholesterol levels and reduce the risk of heart disease. To attain and sustain a healthy weight, it is best to combine a balanced diet with frequent exercise.

Smoking Cessation: Smoking has a negative effect on

your heart's health, including lowering HDL cholesterol. Quitting smoking can improve your cholesterol profile and provide numerous other health benefits. It's never too late to quit, and there are many resources available to help you succeed.

Stress Management: Chronic stress may indirectly influence cholesterol levels by affecting your eating habits and activity levels. Discovering appropriate coping mechanisms for stress, like yoga, meditation, or pastimes, can enhance your life and help you reach your cholesterol reduction objectives.

Sleep: Getting enough sleep is critical to overall wellness. Elevations of LDL cholesterol have been associated with sleep deprivation. For optimal heart health and to help control cholesterol, aim for 7 to 9 hours of good sleep each night.

Alcohol Intake: While moderate alcohol consumption may offer certain health advantages, binge drinking can raise triglyceride and cholesterol levels. If you choose to drink, do so in moderation—up to one drink a day for women and two drinks a day for men.

Incorporating these lifestyle changes can have a profound impact on your cholesterol levels and overall health. You may take charge of your cholesterol and lower your risk of heart disease by concentrating on a diet, exercise routine, weight control, and other healthy habits.

Remember, each positive choice you make adds up to a healthier you. Embrace these lifestyle changes with the same enthusiasm you bring to trying new recipes, and enjoy the journey to a healthier heart.

Chapter 2: Breakfast

Oatmeal with Fresh Berries and Almonds

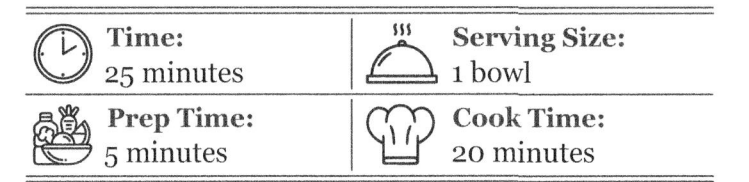

| Time: 25 minutes | Serving Size: 1 bowl |
| Prep Time: 5 minutes | Cook Time: 20 minutes |

Nutrition Information Per Serving (1 bowl):

Calories: 300, Carbohydrates: 45g, Saturated Fat: 0.5g, Protein: 10g, Fat: 8g, Sodium: 30mg, Potassium: 240mg, Fiber: 7g, Sugar: 12g, Vitamin C: 8%, Calcium: 20%, Iron: 15%.

Ingredients:

- 1/2 cup rolled oats
- 1 cup water or almond milk
- 1/2 cup fresh berries (blueberries, strawberries, or raspberries)
- 1 tablespoon sliced almonds
- 1 tablespoon honey or maple syrup (optional)
- 1/4 teaspoon ground cinnamon (optional)

Directions:

1. In a small saucepan, bring 1 cup of water or almond milk to a boil.
2. Stir in 1/2 cup of rolled oats and reduce heat to a simmer.
3. Cook oats for about 10 minutes, stirring occasionally, until they reach your desired consistency.
4. While the oatmeal is cooking, rinse 1/2 cup of fresh berries and slice them if necessary.
5. Once the oatmeal is done, remove from heat and let it sit for 1 minute to thicken further.
6. Transfer the cooked oatmeal to a serving bowl and top with the fresh berries.
7. Sprinkle 1 tablespoon of sliced almonds over the berries.
8. If desired, drizzle honey or maple syrup over the oatmeal for added sweetness.
9. Finish by sprinkling a pinch of ground cinnamon for extra flavor.
10. Stir everything together to combine the flavors and enjoy your heart-healthy breakfast.

Spinach and Mushroom Egg White Omelette

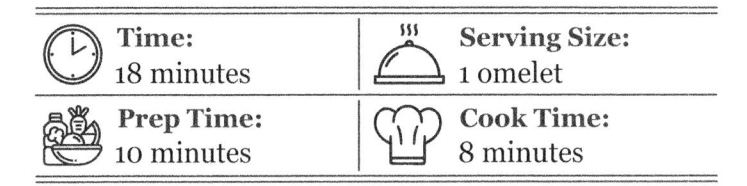

| Time: 18 minutes | Serving Size: 1 omelet |
| Prep Time: 10 minutes | Cook Time: 8 minutes |

Nutrition Information Per Serving (1 omelet):

Calories: 180, Carbohydrates: 6g, Saturated Fat:

0.5g, Protein: 23g, Fat: 8g, Sodium: 400mg, Potassium: 450mg, Fiber: 2g, Sugar: 3g, Vitamin C: 10%, Calcium: 6%, Iron: 10%.

Ingredients:

- 4 large egg whites
- 1 cup fresh spinach, chopped
- 1/2 cup mushrooms, sliced
- 2 tbsp reduced-fat shredded cheddar cheese
- 1 tbsp olive oil
- 1/4 tsp salt
- 1/4 tsp black pepper
- 1/4 tsp dried oregano
- Fresh chives for garnish (optional)

Directions:

1. In a medium bowl, whisk together the egg whites, salt, pepper, and dried oregano until frothy.
2. Heat olive oil in a non-stick skillet over medium heat.
3. Add the sliced mushrooms to the skillet and sauté for about 3 minutes until they are soft and lightly browned.
4. Toss in the chopped spinach and cook for another 2 minutes until the spinach is wilted.
5. Pour the egg white mixture into the skillet over the spinach and mushrooms.
6. Cook for about 2 minutes, then use a spatula to gently lift the edges of the omelette and tilt the pan to allow uncooked egg whites to flow to the edges.
7. When the egg whites are almost set, sprinkle the shredded cheddar cheese on one half of the omelette.
8. Carefully fold the other half over the cheese and press gently with the spatula to seal.
9. Let the omelette cook for another minute until the cheese is melted.
10. Slide the omelette onto a plate, garnish with fresh chives if desired, and serve immediately.

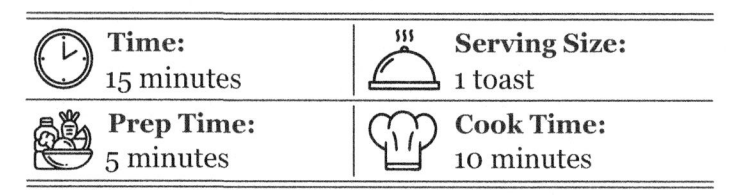

Avocado Toast on Whole Grain Bread

Time: 15 minutes	Serving Size: 1 toast
Prep Time: 5 minutes	Cook Time: 10 minutes

Nutrition Information Per Serving (1 toast):

Calories: 350, Carbohydrates: 37g, Saturated Fat: 3g, Protein: 11g, Fat: 20g, Sodium: 200mg, Potassium: 708mg, Fiber: 10g, Sugar: 4g, Vitamin C: 17%, Calcium: 5%, Iron: 13%.

Ingredients:

- 1 slice whole grain bread
- 1/2 ripe avocado
- 1 tablespoon lemon juice
- 1/4 teaspoon salt
- 1/4 teaspoon black pepper
- 1/4 teaspoon red pepper flakes (optional)
- 1 tablespoon chopped fresh cilantro (optional)

Directions:

1. Toast 1 slice of whole grain bread to your desired level of crispiness.
2. While the bread is toasting, cut the avocado in half, remove the pit, and scoop the flesh into a bowl.
3. Add 1 tablespoon of lemon juice, 1/4 teaspoon of salt, and 1/4 teaspoon of black pepper to the bowl with the avocado.
4. Mash the avocado and seasoning together with a fork until you reach your desired consistency.
5. Once the bread is toasted, spread the mashed avocado evenly over the slice.
6. If desired, sprinkle red pepper flakes on top of the avocado for a bit of heat.

7. Garnish with chopped fresh cilantro for a fresh, herby flavor.
8. Serve immediately and enjoy a heart-healthy, cholesterol-friendly breakfast.

Greek Yogurt Parfait with Honey and Nuts

Time: 15 minutes	Serving Size: 1
Prep Time: 5 minutes	Cook Time: 10 minutes

Nutrition Information Per Serving (1 tall glass):

Calories: 220, Carbohydrates: 28g, Saturated Fat: 0g, Protein: 15g, Fat: 6g, Sodium: 65mg, Potassium: 345mg, Fiber: 3g, Sugar: 20g, Vitamin C: 4%, Calcium: 150mg, Iron: 0.7mg.

Ingredients:

- 1 cup non-fat Greek yogurt
- 2 tablespoons honey
- 1/4 cup mixed nuts (almonds, walnuts, and pistachios), chopped
- 1/2 cup fresh berries (strawberries, blueberries, or raspberries)
- 1 tablespoon ground flaxseed

Directions:

1. In a serving glass or bowl, layer 1/2 cup of non-fat Greek yogurt.
2. Drizzle 1 tablespoon of honey over the yogurt.
3. Sprinkle 2 tablespoons of the mixed nuts on top of the honey.
4. Add 1/4 cup of fresh berries over the nuts.
5. Add another layer of the remaining 1/2 cup of Greek yogurt on top of the berries.
6. Drizzle the remaining 1 tablespoon of honey over the second layer of yogurt.
7. Sprinkle the remaining 2 tablespoons of mixed nuts and add the rest of the berries on top.
8. Garnish the parfait with 1 tablespoon of ground flaxseed for added fiber and omega-3 fatty acids.
9. Serve immediately or refrigerate until ready to eat. Enjoy your nutritious and heart-healthy Greek Yogurt Parfait with Honey and Nuts.

Banana Pancakes with Low-Fat Yogurt Topping

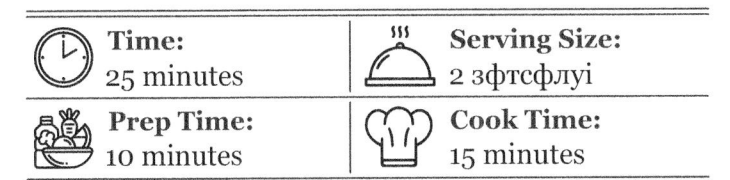

Time: 25 minutes	Serving Size: 2 зфтсфлуі
Prep Time: 10 minutes	Cook Time: 15 minutes

Time: 25 minutes

Serving Size: 2 pancakes

Prep Time: 10 minutes

Cook Time: 15 minutes

Nutrition Information Per Serving (1 pancake):

Calories: 280, Carbohydrates: 45g, Saturated Fat: 1g, Protein: 10g, Fat: 6g, Sodium: 220mg, Potassium: 300mg, Fiber: 4g, Sugar: 18g, Vitamin C: 7%, Calcium: 15%, Iron: 10%.

Ingredients:

- 1 medium ripe banana
- 1 cup whole wheat flour
- 1/2 cup low-fat milk or almond milk
- 1/4 cup low-fat Greek yogurt
- 2 large egg whites
- 1 tablespoon honey
- 1 teaspoon baking powder
- 1/2 teaspoon vanilla extract
- 1/4 teaspoon cinnamon
- Pinch of salt
- Cooking spray or 1

teaspoon olive oil for greasing

Directions:

1. In a large bowl, mash the ripe banana with a fork until smooth.
2. Add the egg whites and vanilla extract to the mashed banana and whisk together until well combined.
3. In a separate bowl, mix together the whole wheat flour, baking powder, cinnamon, and a pinch of salt.
4. Gradually add the dry ingredients to the wet ingredients, alternating with the low-fat milk, and stir until the batter is smooth.
5. Preheat a non-stick skillet or griddle over medium heat and lightly grease with cooking spray or olive oil.
6. Pour 1/4 cup of batter onto the skillet for each pancake. Cook until bubbles form on the surface, then flip and cook until golden brown on the other side, about 2-3 minutes per side.
7. For the topping, mix the low-fat Greek yogurt with honey in a small bowl.
8. Serve the pancakes hot with a dollop of the yogurt-honey mixture on top. Enjoy your heart-healthy Banana Pancakes with Low-Fat Yogurt Topping.

Smoothie Bowl with Chia Seeds and Kiwi

Time: 20 minutes	Serving Size: 1 bowl
Prep Time: 10 minutes	Cook Time: 10 minutes

Nutrition Information Per Serving (1 bowl):

Calories: 330, Carbohydrates: 52g, Saturated Fat: 1g, Protein: 8g, Fat: 12g, Sodium: 55mg, Potassium: 550mg, Fiber: 15g, Sugar: 25g, Vitamin C: 150%, Calcium: 10%, Iron: 15%.

Ingredients:

- 1 cup unsweetened almond milk
- 1/2 ripe banana
- 1 kiwi, peeled and sliced
- 1/2 cup frozen mixed berries
- 1/4 cup rolled oats
- 1 tablespoon chia seeds
- 1 tablespoon honey (optional)
- 1/4 teaspoon vanilla extract
- Toppings: Sliced kiwi, berries, chia seeds, and a drizzle of honey

Directions:

1. In a blender, combine 1 cup of unsweetened almond milk, 1/2 ripe banana, 1 peeled and sliced kiwi, 1/2 cup of frozen mixed berries, 1/4 cup of rolled oats, 1 tablespoon of chia seeds, and 1/4 teaspoon of vanilla extract.
2. Blend on high until smooth and creamy.
3. Pour the smoothie mixture into a bowl.
4. Garnish the smoothie bowl with additional sliced kiwi, berries, and a sprinkle of chia seeds for added texture and nutrients.
5. If desired, drizzle a tablespoon of honey over the top for a touch of sweetness.
6. Serve immediately and enjoy this nutrient-packed, cholesterol-friendly breakfast bowl.

Whole Wheat Veggie Wraps

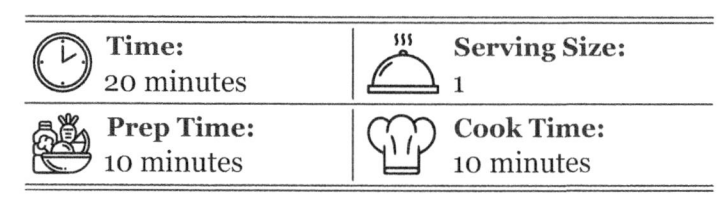

Time: 20 minutes	Serving Size: 1
Prep Time: 10 minutes	Cook Time: 10 minutes

Nutrition Information Per Serving (1

serving unit):

Calories: 260, Carbohydrates: 35g, Saturated Fat: 1g, Protein: 12g, Fat: 8g, Sodium: 320mg, Potassium: 474mg, Fiber: 6g, Sugar: 4g, Vitamin C: 30%, Calcium: 6%, Iron: 15%.

Ingredients:

- 1 whole wheat tortilla (8-inch diameter)
- 1/4 cup hummus
- 1/2 cup spinach leaves, washed and dried
- 1/4 cup grated carrots
- 1/4 cup sliced red bell pepper
- 1/4 cup sliced cucumber
- 1 tablespoon sliced red onion
- 1 tablespoon chopped fresh cilantro
- 1/4 teaspoon ground cumin
- Salt and pepper to taste

Directions:

1. Lay the whole wheat tortilla flat on a clean surface.
2. Spread the hummus evenly over the tortilla, leaving a small border around the edge.
3. Arrange the spinach leaves on top of the hummus.
4. Sprinkle the grated carrots, sliced red bell pepper, and sliced cucumber over the spinach.
5. Add the sliced red onion and fresh cilantro on top of the vegetables.
6. Season with ground cumin, salt, and pepper.
7. Carefully roll the tortilla, starting from one edge and tucking in the sides as you roll to keep the filling secure.
8. Heat a non-stick skillet over medium heat and place the wrap seam-side down to seal it and heat through for about 2 minutes on each side.
9. Slice the wrap in half and serve warm. Enjoy your heart-healthy Whole Wheat Veggie Wrap.

Baked Sweet Potato and Kale Hash

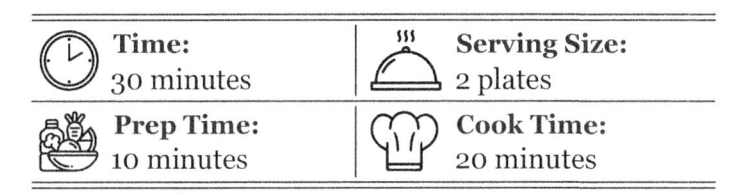

Time: 30 minutes	Serving Size: 2 plates
Prep Time: 10 minutes	Cook Time: 20 minutes

Nutrition Information Per Serving (1 plate):

Calories: 220, Carbohydrates: 30g, Saturated Fat: 0.5g, Protein: 5g, Fat: 8g, Sodium: 170mg, Potassium: 670mg, Fiber: 5g, Sugar: 7g, Vitamin C: 35%, Calcium: 8%, Iron: 10%.

Ingredients:

- 1 large sweet potato, peeled and diced
- 2 cups kale, washed, stems removed and chopped
- 1 small red onion, diced
- 2 cloves garlic, minced
- 1 tablespoon olive oil
- 1/2 teaspoon smoked paprika
- 1/4 teaspoon ground cumin
- Salt and pepper to taste
- Fresh parsley for garnish (optional)

Directions:

1. Preheat your oven to 400°F.
2. In a large mixing bowl, toss the diced sweet potato with olive oil, smoked paprika, ground cumin, salt, and pepper until well coated.
3. Spread the sweet potatoes in a single layer on a baking sheet and bake for 10 minutes.
4. While the sweet potatoes are baking, sauté the diced red onion and minced garlic in a skillet over medium heat until the onions become translucent.
5. After 10 minutes, remove the sweet potatoes from the oven and add the sautéed onions

and garlic. Mix in the chopped kale.

6. Return the baking sheet to the oven and bake for an additional 10 minutes, or until the sweet potatoes are tender and the kale is slightly crispy.

7. Remove from the oven and let it cool for a couple of minutes.

8. Serve the hash warm, garnished with fresh parsley if desired.

Quinoa Porridge with Cinnamon Apples

Time: 25 minutes
Serving Size: 1 bowl
Prep Time: 5 minutes
Cook Time: 20 minutes

Nutrition Information Per Serving (1 bowl):

Calories: 285, Carbohydrates: 55g, Saturated Fat: 0.5g, Protein: 8g, Fat: 5g, Sodium: 10mg, Potassium: 400mg, Fiber: 6g, Sugar: 15g, Vitamin C: 8%, Calcium: 4%, Iron: 15%.

Ingredients:

- 1/2 cup quinoa, rinsed
- 1 cup water
- 1 apple, cored and chopped
- 1/2 teaspoon ground cinnamon
- 1 tablespoon almond slivers
- 1 teaspoon honey or maple syrup (optional)
- A pinch of salt

Directions:

1. In a small saucepan, bring 1 cup of water to a boil. Add a pinch of salt and 1/2 cup of rinsed quinoa. Reduce heat to low, cover, and simmer for 15 minutes or until the quinoa is cooked and the water is absorbed.

2. While the quinoa is cooking, place the chopped apple in a microwave-safe bowl, sprinkle it with ground cinnamon, and microwave for 2 minutes until the apple is soft and warm.

3. Fluff the cooked quinoa with a fork and stir in the cinnamon apples.

4. Transfer the quinoa porridge to a serving bowl.

5. Garnish with almond slivers and drizzle with honey or maple syrup if a sweeter taste is desired.

6. Serve warm and enjoy a hearty, nutritious start to your day with this Quinoa Porridge with Cinnamon Apples.

Low-Fat Cottage Cheese with Pineapple

Time: 15 minutes
Serving Size: 1
Prep Time: 5 minutes
Cook Time: 10 minutes

Nutrition Information Per Serving (1 glass):

Calories: 180, Carbohydrates: 16g, Saturated Fat: 0.7g, Protein: 14g, Fat: 2g, Sodium: 500mg, Potassium: 210mg, Fiber: 1g, Sugar: 14g, Vitamin C: 50%, Calcium: 8%, Iron: 2%.

Ingredients:

- 1/2 cup low-fat cottage cheese
- 1/2 cup chopped fresh pineapple
- 1 tablespoon chopped almonds
- 1 teaspoon honey (optional)
- A pinch of cinnamon (optional)

Directions:

1. Place the low-fat cottage cheese in a serving bowl.

2. Top the cottage cheese with the freshly chopped pineapple.

3. Sprinkle the chopped almonds over the pineapple for added texture and a nutty flavor.

4. If desired, drizzle honey over the top for a touch of sweetness.

5. Finish with a pinch of cinnamon for a warm, spicy note.

6. Serve immediately as a refreshing and nutritious start to your day.

Vegan Tofu Scramble with Tomatoes

Time: 20 minutes	Serving Size: 2
Prep Time: 5 minutes	Cook Time: 15 minutes

Nutrition Information Per Serving (1 plate):

Calories: 250, Carbohydrates: 15g, Saturated Fat: 1g, Protein: 18g, Fat: 14g, Sodium: 320mg, Potassium: 200mg, Fiber: 4g, Sugar: 3g, Vitamin C: 25%, Calcium: 35%, Iron: 15%.

Ingredients:

- 1 block (14 oz) firm tofu, drained and crumbled
- 1 tablespoon olive oil
- 1/2 cup cherry tomatoes, halved
- 1/4 cup red bell pepper, diced
- 1/4 cup yellow bell pepper, diced
- 1/4 cup onion, finely chopped
- 1 clove garlic, minced
- 1 teaspoon turmeric
- 1/2 teaspoon cumin
- 1/4 teaspoon paprika
- Salt and black pepper to taste
- Fresh cilantro or parsley for garnish (optional)

Directions:

1. Heat olive oil in a non-stick skillet over medium heat.

2. Add the onion and garlic to the skillet and sauté until the onions are translucent, about 3 minutes.

3. Stir in the red and yellow bell peppers and cook for another 2 minutes.

4. Crumble the tofu into the skillet, then sprinkle in the turmeric, cumin, paprika, salt, and black pepper. Mix well to combine all the ingredients and evenly distribute the spices.

5. Let the tofu cook without stirring for a couple of minutes to allow it to brown slightly, then stir and cook for another 5 minutes.

6. Add the cherry tomatoes and cook for an additional 2-3 minutes, until the tomatoes are just starting to soften.

7. Remove from heat, garnish with fresh cilantro or parsley if desired, and serve hot.

Overnight Chia Seed Pudding

Time: 15 minutes	Serving Size: 1 glass
Prep Time: 5 minutes	Cook Time: 10 minutes

Nutrition Information Per Serving (1 glass):

Calories: 200, Carbohydrates: 24g, Saturated Fat: 0g, Protein: 6g, Fat: 9g, Sodium: 30mg, Potassium: 150mg, Fiber: 10g, Sugar: 8g, Vitamin C: 0%, Calcium: 25%, Iron: 15%.

Ingredients:

- 3 tablespoons chia seeds
- 1 cup unsweetened almond milk
- 1/2 teaspoon vanilla extract
- 1 tablespoon maple syrup
- 1/2 cup mixed berries (strawberries, blueberries, raspberries)
- A pinch of ground cinnamon (optional)

Directions:

1. In a mason jar or a bowl, combine 3

tablespoons of chia seeds with 1 cup of unsweetened almond milk.

2. Add 1/2 teaspoon of vanilla extract and 1 tablespoon of maple syrup to the mixture. Stir well to combine.

3. If desired, add a pinch of ground cinnamon for additional flavor.

4. Cover the jar or bowl with a lid or plastic wrap and refrigerate overnight or for at least 6 hours.

5. The next morning, give the chia seed pudding a good stir. If the pudding is too thick, add a little more almond milk until you reach the desired consistency.

6. Top the pudding with 1/2 cup of mixed berries before serving.

7. Enjoy this Overnight Chia Seed Pudding as a heart-healthy breakfast option.

Whole Grain Blueberry Muffins

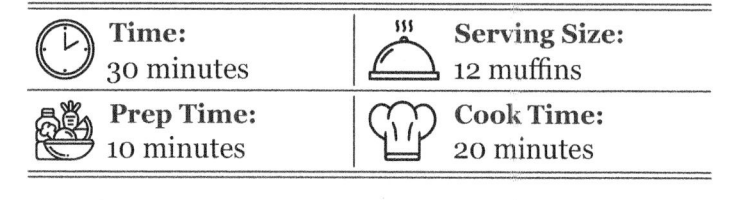

⏰	**Time:** 30 minutes	🍲	**Serving Size:** 12 muffins
🥗	**Prep Time:** 10 minutes	👨‍🍳	**Cook Time:** 20 minutes

Nutrition Information Per Serving (1 muffin):

Calories: 150, Carbohydrates: 27g, Saturated Fat: 0.5g, Protein: 4g, Fat: 3g, Sodium: 210mg, Potassium: 77mg, Fiber: 4g, Sugar: 7g, Vitamin C: 2%, Calcium: 20mg, Iron: 1.2mg.

Ingredients:

- 1 cup whole wheat flour
- 3/4 cup rolled oats
- 1/2 cup light brown sugar
- 1 tablespoon baking powder
- 1/2 teaspoon baking soda
- 1/4 teaspoon salt
- 1 teaspoon ground cinnamon
- 1 cup unsweetened applesauce
- 1/2 cup non-fat milk
- 1/4 cup unsweetened almond milk
- 2 large egg whites
- 1 teaspoon vanilla extract
- 1 cup fresh blueberries

Directions:

1. Preheat your oven to 375°F and line a muffin tin with paper liners or spray with non-stick cooking spray.

2. In a large bowl, whisk together the whole wheat flour, rolled oats, light brown sugar, baking powder, baking soda, salt, and ground cinnamon.

3. In a separate bowl, mix the unsweetened applesauce, non-fat milk, unsweetened almond milk, egg whites, and vanilla extract until well combined.

4. Pour the wet ingredients into the dry ingredients and stir until just combined, being careful not to overmix.

5. Gently fold in the fresh blueberries.

6. Divide the batter evenly among the prepared muffin cups, filling each about two-thirds full.

7. Bake in the preheated oven for 20 minutes, or until a toothpick inserted into the center of a muffin comes out clean.

8. Allow the muffins to cool in the pan for 5 minutes before transferring them to a wire rack to cool completely.

Chapter 3: Snacks and Appetizers

Carrot and Cucumber Sticks with Hummus

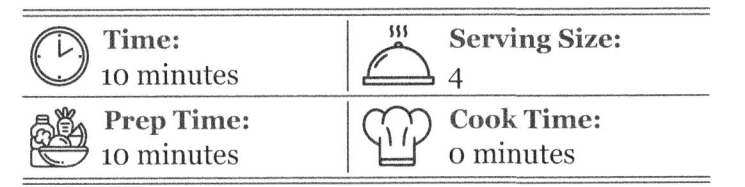

Time: 10 minutes	Serving Size: 4
Prep Time: 10 minutes	Cook Time: 0 minutes

Nutrition Information Per Serving (1 plate):

Calories: 180, Carbohydrates: 20g, Saturated Fat: 1g, Protein: 6g, Fat: 10g, Sodium: 200mg, Potassium: 360mg, Fiber: 5g, Sugar: 4g, Vitamin C: 8%, Calcium: 4%, Iron: 12%.

Ingredients:

- 2 large carrots, peeled and cut into sticks
- 2 medium cucumbers, cut into sticks
- 1 cup hummus, store-bought or homemade
- 1 tablespoon olive oil
- 1/2 teaspoon paprika (optional for garnish)
- 1/4 teaspoon cumin
- A pinch of salt
- Fresh parsley or cilantro for garnish (optional)

Directions:

1. Wash the carrots and cucumbers thoroughly. Peel the carrots and cut both vegetables into stick shapes, about 3 inches long and 1/4 inch thick.
2. Prepare the hummus by blending chickpeas, olive oil, cumin, and a pinch of salt until smooth. If using store-bought hummus, you can skip this step.
3. Arrange the carrot and cucumber sticks on a serving platter.
4. Place the hummus in a small bowl and sprinkle paprika over it for a touch of color and a hint of smoky flavor, if desired.
5. Garnish with fresh parsley or cilantro for an additional fresh taste and presentation, if you like.
6. Serve the carrot and cucumber sticks alongside the bowl of hummus for dipping.

Roasted Chickpeas with Paprika

Time: 40 minutes	Serving Size: 4
Prep Time: 5 minutes	Cook Time: 35 minutes

Nutrition Information Per Serving (1 bowl):

Calories: 146, Carbohydrates: 22g, Saturated Fat: 0.3g, Protein: 6g, Fat: 4g, Sodium: 304mg, Potassium: 291mg, Fiber: 6g, Sugar: 4g, Vitamin C: 2%, Calcium: 5%, Iron: 10%.

Ingredients:

- 1 can (15 oz) chickpeas, drained and rinsed
- 1 tablespoon olive oil
- 1/2 teaspoon smoked paprika
- 1/4 teaspoon garlic powder
- 1/4 teaspoon onion powder

- 1/4 teaspoon sea salt
- 1/8 teaspoon black pepper
- 1/4 teaspoon cayenne pepper (optional for extra heat)

Directions:

1. Preheat your oven to 400°F.
2. Pat the chickpeas dry with paper towels, removing any loose skins.
3. In a bowl, toss the chickpeas with 1 tablespoon of olive oil until they are evenly coated.
4. Sprinkle the smoked paprika, garlic powder, onion powder, sea salt, black pepper, and cayenne pepper over the chickpeas. Stir until the chickpeas are evenly seasoned.
5. Spread the chickpeas out in an even layer on a baking sheet lined with parchment paper.
6. Roast in the preheated oven for 35 minutes, shaking the pan or stirring the chickpeas halfway through, until they are golden and crispy.
7. Remove from the oven and let them cool slightly before serving. They will continue to crisp up as they cool.
8. Serve the roasted chickpeas as a crunchy, flavorful snack or appetizer.

Baked Kale Chips

Time: 30 minutes	Serving Size: 4
Prep Time: 10 minutes	Cook Time: 20 minutes

Nutrition Information Per Serving (1 bowl):

Calories: 50, Carbohydrates: 10g, Saturated Fat: 0g, Protein: 2g, Fat: 1g, Sodium: 30mg, Potassium: 299mg, Fiber: 2g, Sugar: 0g, Vitamin C: 134%, Calcium: 90mg, Iron: 1mg.

Ingredients:

- 1 bunch kale, washed and dried
- 1 tablespoon olive oil
- 1/4 teaspoon sea salt
- 1/2 teaspoon paprika
- 1/4 teaspoon garlic powder

Directions:

1. Preheat your oven to 300°F.
2. Remove the kale leaves from the thick stems and tear into bite-sized pieces.
3. In a large bowl, gently toss the kale with olive oil, sea salt, paprika, and garlic powder until the leaves are lightly coated.
4. Arrange the kale pieces in a single layer on a baking sheet lined with parchment paper.
5. Bake in the preheated oven for 10 minutes, then turn the leaves over and bake for another 10 minutes, or until the edges are slightly browned and the kale is crispy.
6. Let the kale chips cool for a few minutes before serving to allow them to crisp up further.

Almonds and Walnuts Trail Mix

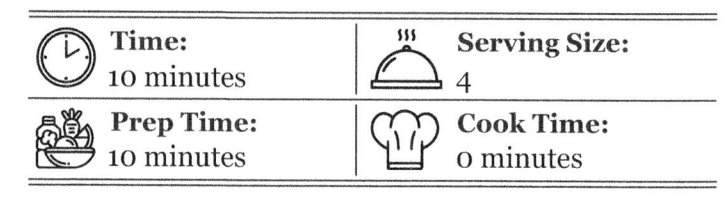

Time: 10 minutes	Serving Size: 4
Prep Time: 10 minutes	Cook Time: 0 minutes

Nutrition Information Per Serving (1 bowl):

Calories: 210, Carbohydrates: 9g, Saturated Fat: 1.5g, Protein: 6g, Fat: 18g, Sodium: 0mg, Potassium: 250mg, Fiber: 4g, Sugar: 2g, Vitamin C: 0%, Calcium: 8%, Iron: 10%.

Ingredients:

- 1/2 cup raw almonds
- 1/2 cup raw walnuts

- 1/4 cup pumpkin seeds
- 1/4 cup sunflower seeds
- 2 tablespoons dried cranberries
- 2 tablespoons raisins
- 1/4 teaspoon ground cinnamon
- A pinch of sea salt

Directions:

1. In a large mixing bowl, combine the raw almonds, walnuts, pumpkin seeds, and sunflower seeds.
2. Add the dried cranberries and raisins to the nut and seed mixture.
3. Sprinkle the ground cinnamon and a pinch of sea salt over the mixture.
4. Toss all ingredients together until they are well mixed and evenly coated with the cinnamon and salt.
5. Divide the trail mix into individual portions or store in an airtight container to maintain freshness.
6. Enjoy this heart-healthy trail mix as a snack on the go or as a nutritious appetizer.

Stuffed Bell Peppers with Quinoa

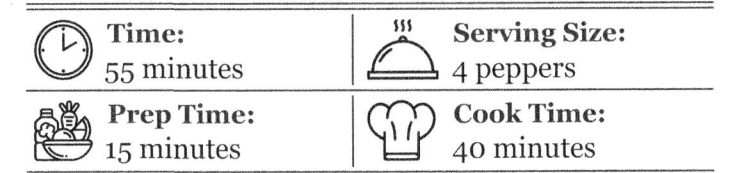

Time: 55 minutes
Serving Size: 4 peppers
Prep Time: 15 minutes
Cook Time: 40 minutes

Nutrition Information Per Serving (1 pepper):

Calories: 229, Carbohydrates: 37g, Saturated Fat: 0.5g, Protein: 9g, Fat: 5g, Sodium: 297mg, Potassium: 676mg, Fiber: 7g, Sugar: 8g, Vitamin C: 169%, Calcium: 5%, Iron: 16%.

Ingredients:

- 4 medium bell peppers, tops cut off and seeds removed
- 1 cup cooked quinoa
- 1/2 cup black beans, rinsed and drained
- 1/2 cup corn kernels, fresh or frozen
- 1/2 cup diced tomatoes
- 1/4 cup chopped red onion
- 1/4 cup chopped cilantro
- 1 teaspoon chili powder
- 1/2 teaspoon cumin
- 1/2 teaspoon garlic powder
- 1/2 teaspoon paprika
- Sea salt and black pepper to taste
- 1/4 cup shredded low-fat cheddar cheese (optional)

Directions:

1. Preheat your oven to 350°F.
2. In a large bowl, mix together the cooked quinoa, black beans, corn kernels, diced tomatoes, red onion, and cilantro.
3. Season the mixture with chili powder, cumin, garlic powder, paprika, sea salt, and black pepper. Stir until all ingredients are well combined.
4. Spoon the quinoa mixture into each bell pepper cavity until they are all evenly filled.
5. Place the stuffed peppers upright in a baking dish. If using cheese, sprinkle the tops of each pepper with shredded low-fat cheddar cheese.
6. Pour a small amount of water into the bottom of the baking dish to help steam the peppers, about a 1/4 inch deep.
7. Cover the dish with aluminum foil and bake in the preheated oven for about 35-40 minutes, or until the peppers are tender.
8. Remove the foil and bake for an additional 5 minutes if you added cheese, until the cheese is melted and slightly golden.
9. Serve the stuffed bell peppers warm as a nutritious and satisfying snack or appetizer.

Edamame with Sea Salt

Time: 15 minutes	Serving Size: 4
Prep Time: 5 minutes	Cook Time: 10 minutes

Nutrition Information Per Serving (1 bowl):

Calories: 122, Carbohydrates: 9g, Saturated Fat: 0.5g, Protein: 11g, Fat: 5g, Sodium: 120mg, Potassium: 482mg, Fiber: 4g, Sugar: 2g, Vitamin C: 10%, Calcium: 5%, Iron: 13%.

Ingredients:

- 16 oz (1 lb) frozen edamame in the pod
- 1 tablespoon sea salt

Directions:

1. Bring a large pot of water to a boil over high heat.
2. Add the frozen edamame and cook for 5 minutes, or until the edamame are tender and bright green.
3. Drain the edamame in a colander and rinse with cold water to stop the cooking process.
4. Pat the edamame dry with a clean kitchen towel or paper towels.
5. Sprinkle the edamame with sea salt, tossing to ensure even coverage.
6. Serve the edamame warm or at room temperature as a healthy and satisfying snack.

Fruit Kebabs with Yogurt Dip

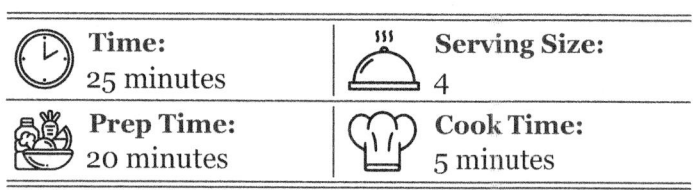

Time: 25 minutes	Serving Size: 4
Prep Time: 20 minutes	Cook Time: 5 minutes

Nutrition Information Per Serving (1 fruit kebab):

Calories: 150, Carbohydrates: 28g, Saturated Fat: 0.1g, Protein: 4g, Fat: 2g, Sodium: 45mg, Potassium: 325mg, Fiber: 3g, Sugar: 20g, Vitamin C: 75%, Calcium: 10%, Iron: 5%.

Ingredients:

- 1 cup strawberries, hulled and halved
- 1 cup cantaloupe, cut into cubes or balls
- 1 cup pineapple, cut into cubes
- 1 cup kiwi, peeled and sliced
- 8 wooden skewers
- 1 cup low-fat Greek yogurt
- 1 tablespoon honey
- 1/2 teaspoon vanilla extract
- A pinch of cinnamon (optional)

Directions:

1. Prepare the fruit by washing and cutting them into bite-sized pieces as described in the ingredients list.
2. Thread the strawberries, cantaloupe, pineapple, and kiwi onto the wooden skewers, alternating the fruit to create a colorful pattern.
3. In a small mixing bowl, combine the low-fat Greek yogurt, honey, vanilla extract, and a pinch of cinnamon if desired. Stir the mixture until it is smooth and well combined.
4. Arrange the fruit kebabs on a serving platter and serve with the yogurt dip on the side.
5. Enjoy these refreshing fruit kebabs as a healthy snack or appetizer, perfect for a low-cholesterol diet.

Zucchini Fritters

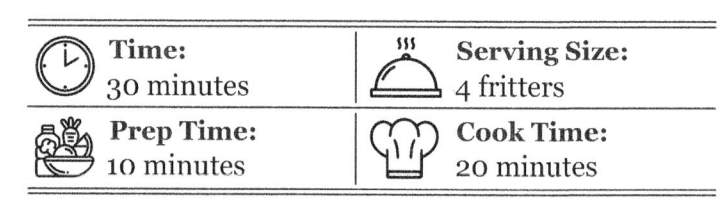

Time: 30 minutes	Serving Size: 4 fritters
Prep Time: 10 minutes	Cook Time: 20 minutes

Nutrition Information Per Serving (1

fritter):

Calories: 124, Carbohydrates: 17g, Saturated Fat: 0.7g, Protein: 6g, Fat: 4g, Sodium: 58mg, Potassium: 470mg, Fiber: 2.5g, Sugar: 4g, Vitamin C: 35%, Calcium: 6%, Iron: 8%.

Ingredients:

- 2 medium zucchinis, grated
- 1/4 cup whole wheat flour
- 1/4 cup grated Parmesan cheese
- 1 large egg
- 2 tablespoons chopped green onions
- 1 teaspoon dried oregano
- 1/4 teaspoon garlic powder
- 1/4 teaspoon ground black pepper
- Olive oil cooking spray

Directions:

1. Place the grated zucchini in a colander, sprinkle with a pinch of salt, and let it sit to draw out the moisture for about 10 minutes. Squeeze out the excess water.
2. In a large bowl, combine the drained zucchini, whole wheat flour, grated Parmesan cheese, egg, green onions, dried oregano, garlic powder, and black pepper. Mix well to form a batter.
3. Heat a non-stick skillet over medium heat and coat with olive oil cooking spray.
4. Scoop a heaping tablespoon of the zucchini mixture into the skillet, flattening it slightly to form a fritter. Cook for about 3-4 minutes on each side or until golden brown and cooked through.
5. Transfer the fritters to a plate lined with paper towels to absorb any excess oil.
6. Serve warm, optionally with a side of low-fat yogurt or a light sour cream dip.

Baked Apple Chips

Time: 1 hour 15 minutes	**Serving Size:** 4
Prep Time: 15 minutes	**Cook Time:** 1 hour

Nutrition Information Per Serving (1 plate):

Calories: 95, Carbohydrates: 25g, Saturated Fat: 0g, Protein: 0.5g, Fat: 0.3g, Sodium: 2mg, Potassium: 195mg, Fiber: 4.4g, Sugar: 19g, Vitamin C: 8.4%, Calcium: 1.2%, Iron: 1.5%.

Ingredients:

- 2 large apples, any sweet variety
- 1 teaspoon ground cinnamon
- Cooking spray (optional)

Directions:

1. Preheat your oven to 200°F.
2. Wash the apples and slice them thinly using a mandoline slicer or a sharp knife, removing the seeds and core.
3. Arrange the apple slices in a single layer on a baking sheet lined with parchment paper. If you don't have parchment paper, lightly spray the baking sheet with cooking spray to prevent sticking.
4. Sprinkle the apple slices with ground cinnamon to add flavor without adding cholesterol or sodium.
5. Bake in the preheated oven for 1 hour. After 1 hour, flip the apple slices over and continue baking for another hour or until the apple chips are crisp and dry to the touch.
6. Remove the apple chips from the oven and let them cool completely on the baking sheet. They will continue to crisp up as they cool.
7. Once cooled, serve the apple chips as a crunchy, heart-healthy snack. Store any leftovers in an airtight container to maintain their crispness.

CHAPTER 3: SNACKS AND APPETIZERS

Caprese Salad Skewers

	Time: 15 minutes		Serving Size: 4 skewers
	Prep Time: 15 minutes		Cook Time: 0 minutes

Nutrition Information Per Serving (1 skewer):

Calories: 80, Carbohydrates: 6g, Saturated Fat: 3g, Protein: 5g, Fat: 5g, Sodium: 210mg, Potassium: 201mg, Fiber: 1g, Sugar: 4g, Vitamin C: 16%, Calcium: 15%, Iron: 3%.

Ingredients:

- 16 cherry tomatoes
- 16 small balls fresh mozzarella cheese (bocconcini)
- 16 fresh basil leaves
- 2 tablespoons balsamic glaze
- 1 tablespoon extra virgin olive oil
- 1/4 teaspoon salt
- 1/4 teaspoon freshly ground black pepper
- 16 toothpicks or small skewers

Directions:

1. Wash the cherry tomatoes and basil leaves, then pat them dry with paper towels.
2. Assemble the skewers by starting with a cherry tomato, followed by a basil leaf, and then a mozzarella ball. Repeat the process until all ingredients are used.
3. Arrange the Caprese skewers on a serving platter.
4. In a small bowl, whisk together the balsamic glaze, extra virgin olive oil, salt, and pepper.
5. Drizzle the balsamic mixture over the skewers just before serving.
6. Serve immediately as a fresh, flavorful appetizer that's perfect for a low-cholesterol diet.

Rice Cakes with Avocado Spread

	Time: 10 minutes		Serving Size: 2
	Prep Time: 10 minutes		Cook Time: 0 minutes

Nutrition Information Per Serving (1 rice cake):

Calories: 214, Carbohydrates: 31g, Saturated Fat: 1.4g, Protein: 4g, Fat: 9g, Sodium: 100mg, Potassium: 487mg, Fiber: 7g, Sugar: 1g, Vitamin C: 12%, Calcium: 3%, Iron: 5%.

Ingredients:

- 2 plain rice cakes
- 1 ripe avocado
- 1 teaspoon lemon juice
- 1/4 teaspoon salt
- 1/4 teaspoon black pepper
- 1/2 teaspoon chia seeds
- 2 tablespoons diced tomato
- 1 tablespoon chopped cilantro (optional)

Directions:

1. In a small bowl, mash the ripe avocado with a fork until it reaches a smooth consistency.
2. Stir in the lemon juice, salt, and black pepper into the mashed avocado to create the spread.
3. Spread half of the avocado mixture onto each rice cake evenly.
4. Sprinkle the chia seeds over the avocado spread for added texture and nutrients.
5. Top each rice cake with diced tomato and, if desired, a sprinkle of chopped cilantro for a fresh flavor.
6. Serve immediately as a delicious and cholesterol-friendly snack or appetizer. Enjoy your heart-healthy Rice Cakes with Avocado Spread!

Roasted Brussel Sprouts with Balsamic Glaze

| Time: 40 minutes | Serving Size: 4 |
| Prep Time: 10 minutes | Cook Time: 30 minutes |

Nutrition Information Per Serving (1 bowl):

Calories: 122, Carbohydrates: 17g, Saturated Fat: 0.5g, Protein: 4g, Fat: 5g, Sodium: 33mg, Potassium: 441mg, Fiber: 4g, Sugar: 5g, Vitamin C: 124%, Calcium: 4%, Iron: 10%.

Ingredients:

- 1 lb Brussels sprouts, trimmed and halved
- 1 tablespoon olive oil
- 1/4 teaspoon salt
- 1/4 teaspoon black pepper
- 2 tablespoons balsamic vinegar
- 1 teaspoon honey

Directions:

1. Preheat your oven to 400°F.
2. In a large bowl, toss the Brussels sprouts with olive oil, salt, and black pepper until they are evenly coated.
3. Spread the Brussels sprouts on a baking sheet in a single layer, ensuring they are not overcrowded.
4. Roast in the preheated oven for about 20 minutes, then stir the Brussels sprouts for even cooking.
5. Continue roasting for another 10 minutes or until they are tender and the edges start to caramelize.
6. While the Brussels sprouts are roasting, prepare the glaze by whisking together balsamic vinegar and honey in a small bowl.
7. Once the Brussels sprouts are done, drizzle the balsamic glaze over them while they are still warm and toss to coat evenly.
8. Serve the roasted Brussels sprouts with balsamic glaze as a delicious and heart-healthy appetizer.

Sweet Potato Wedges with Low-Fat Greek Yogurt Dip

| Time: 35 minutes | Serving Size: 4 |
| Prep Time: 10 minutes | Cook Time: 25 minutes |

Nutrition Information Per Serving (1 bowl):

Calories: 150, Carbohydrates: 23g, Saturated Fat: 0.5g, Protein: 6g, Fat: 3g, Sodium: 80mg, Potassium: 438mg, Fiber: 3g, Sugar: 7g, Vitamin C: 22%, Calcium: 6%, Iron: 5%

Ingredients:

- 2 large sweet potatoes, cut into wedges
- 1 tablespoon olive oil
- 1/2 teaspoon smoked paprika
- 1/4 teaspoon garlic powder
- 1/4 teaspoon onion powder
- Salt and pepper to taste
- 1 cup low-fat Greek yogurt
- 1 tablespoon fresh lemon juice
- 1 tablespoon chopped chives
- 1 clove garlic, minced

Directions:

1. Preheat your oven to 425°F.
2. Toss the sweet potato wedges with olive oil, smoked paprika, garlic powder, onion powder, salt, and pepper until they are evenly coated.
3. Spread the wedges on a baking sheet in a single layer.
4. Roast in the preheated oven for 25 minutes,

or until the wedges are tender and golden brown, turning halfway through the cooking time.

5. While the sweet potatoes are roasting, prepare the dip by combining the low-fat Greek yogurt, lemon juice, chopped chives, and minced garlic in a small bowl.

6. Chill the yogurt dip in the refrigerator until the sweet potato wedges are ready to be served.

7. Serve the sweet potato wedges warm with the chilled Greek yogurt dip on the side.

Chapter 4: Poultry Dishes

Grilled Chicken Salad with Mixed Greens

Time: 25 minutes	Serving Size: 4
Prep Time: 15 minutes	Cook Time: 10 minutes

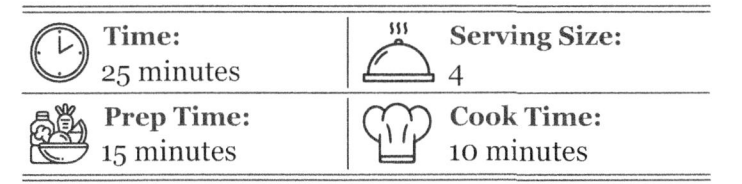

Nutrition Information Per Serving (1 plate):

Calories: 220, Carbohydrates: 8g, Saturated Fat: 1g, Protein: 35g, Fat: 6g, Sodium: 150mg, Potassium: 650mg, Fiber: 2g, Sugar: 4g, Vitamin C: 25%, Calcium: 5%, Iron: 12%.

Ingredients:

- 4 boneless, skinless chicken breasts (about 4 oz each)
- 1 tablespoon olive oil
- 1/2 teaspoon garlic powder
- 1/2 teaspoon dried oregano
- Salt and pepper to taste
- 8 cups mixed greens (lettuce, spinach, arugula)
- 1 cup cherry tomatoes, halved
- 1/2 red onion, thinly sliced
- 1/4 cup balsamic vinaigrette
- 1/4 cup shaved Parmesan cheese

Directions:

1. Preheat the grill to medium-high heat.
2. Brush chicken breasts with olive oil and season with garlic powder, oregano, salt, and pepper.
3. Grill chicken for about 5 minutes on each side, or until the internal temperature reaches 165°F and the juices run clear.
4. Remove chicken from the grill and let it rest for a few minutes before slicing it thinly.
5. In a large bowl, combine mixed greens, cherry tomatoes, and red onion.
6. Drizzle the salad with balsamic vinaigrette and toss to coat the greens evenly.
7. Divide the salad among four plates and top each with grilled chicken slices and shaved Parmesan cheese.
8. Serve the Grilled Chicken Salad with Mixed Greens immediately for a fresh and satisfying meal.

Turkey Lettuce Wraps

Time: 20 minutes	Serving Size: 4
Prep Time: 10 minutes	Cook Time: 10 minutes

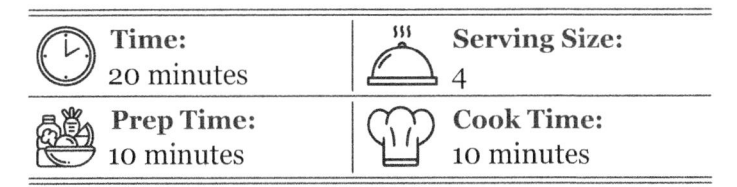

Nutrition Information Per Serving (1 serving unit):

Calories: 248, Carbohydrates: 12g, Saturated Fat: 1.2g, Protein: 26g, Fat: 12g, Sodium: 412mg, Potassium: 340mg, Fiber: 3g, Sugar: 4g, Vitamin C: 5%, Calcium: 4%, Iron: 15%.

Ingredients:

- 1 pound ground turkey breast
- 1 tablespoon olive oil
- 1 medium onion, diced
- 2 cloves garlic, minced
- 1 red bell pepper, diced
- 1 tablespoon low-sodium soy sauce
- 1 tablespoon hoisin sauce
- 1 teaspoon rice vinegar
- 1/4 teaspoon ground ginger
- 1 head iceberg lettuce, leaves separated
- 1 carrot, shredded
- 1/4 cup chopped cilantro

Directions:

1. Heat the olive oil in a skillet over medium heat.
2. Add the diced onion and minced garlic to the skillet and sauté until the onion is translucent.
3. Incorporate the ground turkey breast into the skillet, breaking it apart with a spatula. Cook until the turkey is no longer pink.
4. Stir in the diced red bell pepper, low-sodium soy sauce, hoisin sauce, rice vinegar, and ground ginger. Cook for an additional 5 minutes, allowing the flavors to meld.
5. Remove from heat and let the turkey mixture cool slightly.
6. Arrange the iceberg lettuce leaves on a platter, spoon the turkey mixture into the center of each leaf.
7. Garnish each wrap with shredded carrot and chopped cilantro.
8. Serve the turkey lettuce wraps immediately, encouraging diners to eat them with their hands like tacos.

Chicken and Vegetable Stir-Fry

Time: 30 minutes
Serving Size: 4
Prep Time: 15 minutes
Cook Time: 15 minutes

Nutrition Information Per Serving (1 bowl):

Calories: 275, Carbohydrates: 18g, Saturated Fat: 1g, Protein: 27g, Fat: 11g, Sodium: 300mg, Potassium: 700mg, Fiber: 4g, Sugar: 8g, Vitamin C: 120%, Calcium: 4%, Iron: 10%.

Ingredients:

- 1 pound boneless, skinless chicken breast, cut into bite-sized pieces
- 2 tablespoons olive oil, divided
- 1 tablespoon low-sodium soy sauce
- 1 tablespoon hoisin sauce
- 2 teaspoons sesame oil
- 1 tablespoon cornstarch
- 1/2 cup low-sodium chicken broth
- 1 bell pepper, sliced
- 1 cup broccoli florets
- 1 carrot, julienned
- 1/2 cup snow peas
- 1 tablespoon grated ginger
- 2 cloves garlic, minced
- 1/4 cup sliced green onions
- Salt and pepper to taste

Directions:

1. In a bowl, whisk together the low-sodium soy sauce, hoisin sauce, sesame oil, cornstarch, and low-sodium chicken broth. Set aside.
2. Heat 1 tablespoon of olive oil in a large skillet or wok over medium-high heat.
3. Season the chicken pieces with salt and pepper, then add to the skillet. Cook until the chicken is browned and cooked through, about 5-7 minutes. Remove the chicken and set aside.
4. Add the remaining tablespoon of olive oil to

the skillet. Stir-fry the bell pepper, broccoli, carrot, and snow peas until they are just tender, about 3-4 minutes.

5. Add the grated ginger and minced garlic to the vegetables and cook for an additional minute.

6. Return the chicken to the skillet and pour the sauce mixture over the chicken and vegetables.

7. Cook for another 2-3 minutes, until the sauce has thickened and everything is heated through.

8. Garnish with sliced green onions before serving.

Baked Chicken with Herbs and Lemon

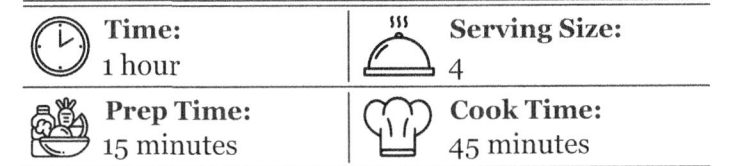

Time: 1 hour	Serving Size: 4
Prep Time: 15 minutes	Cook Time: 45 minutes

Nutrition Information Per Serving (1 serving unit):

Calories: 375, Carbohydrates: 5g, Saturated Fat: 2g, Protein: 30g, Fat: 25g, Sodium: 200mg, Potassium: 400mg, Fiber: 1g, Sugar: 1g, Vitamin C: 20%, Calcium: 3%, Iron: 8%.

Ingredients:

- 4 boneless, skinless chicken breasts
- 2 tablespoons olive oil
- 4 garlic cloves, minced
- 1 tablespoon fresh rosemary, chopped
- 1 tablespoon fresh thyme, chopped
- 1 lemon, sliced
- Salt and pepper to taste

Directions:

1. Preheat your oven to 375°F.

2. In a small bowl, mix together olive oil, minced garlic, rosemary, thyme, salt, and pepper.

3. Lay the chicken breasts in a baking dish and rub them evenly with the herb mixture.

4. Place lemon slices on top of the chicken breasts.

5. Bake in the preheated oven for 45 minutes, or until the chicken is cooked through and reaches an internal temperature of 165°F.

6. Once cooked, let the chicken rest for a few minutes before serving.

7. Serve the baked chicken with a side of steamed vegetables or a salad for a complete meal.

Turkey Quinoa Meatballs

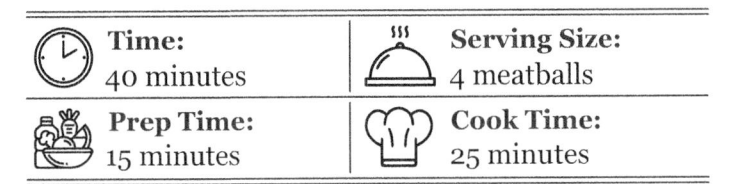

Time: 40 minutes	Serving Size: 4 meatballs
Prep Time: 15 minutes	Cook Time: 25 minutes

Nutrition Information Per Serving (1 meatball):

Calories: 320, Carbohydrates: 22g, Saturated Fat: 1.5g, Protein: 29g, Fat: 12g, Sodium: 480mg, Potassium: 270mg, Fiber: 3g, Sugar: 1g, Vitamin C: 0%, Calcium: 4%, Iron: 18%.

Ingredients:

- 1 pound ground turkey breast
- 1 cup cooked quinoa
- 1/4 cup finely chopped onion
- 2 cloves garlic, minced
- 1 egg, beaten
- 2 tablespoons chopped fresh parsley
- 1 teaspoon dried oregano
- 1/2 teaspoon salt
- 1/4 teaspoon black pepper
- 1/2 cup low-sodium chicken broth
- 1 tablespoon olive oil

Directions:

1. Preheat the oven to 375°F.
2. In a large bowl, combine the ground turkey, cooked quinoa, chopped onion, minced garlic, beaten egg, chopped parsley, dried oregano, salt, and black pepper. Mix well until all ingredients are evenly distributed.
3. Shape the mixture into 1-inch meatballs and place them on a baking sheet lined with parchment paper.
4. In a small saucepan, bring the chicken broth to a simmer.
5. Brush each meatball with olive oil, then spoon a little of the hot chicken broth over the top of each meatball.
6. Bake in the preheated oven for 25 minutes, or until the meatballs are cooked through and have a slight golden color.
7. Serve the turkey quinoa meatballs with a side of steamed vegetables or over a bed of mixed greens for a complete meal.

Chicken and Broccoli Alfredo (with Whole Wheat Pasta)

Time: 35 minutes	Serving Size: 4
Prep Time: 10 minutes	Cook Time: 25 minutes

Nutrition Information Per Serving (1 bowl):

Calories: 330, Carbohydrates: 35g, Saturated Fat: 2g, Protein: 29g, Fat: 9g, Sodium: 190mg, Potassium: 520mg, Fiber: 6g, Sugar: 3g, Vitamin C: 85%, Calcium: 15%, Iron: 10%.

Ingredients:

- 8 ounces whole wheat pasta
- 1 pound boneless, skinless chicken breast, cut into strips
- 2 cups broccoli florets
- 2 teaspoons olive oil
- 1 cup low-sodium chicken broth
- 1 cup low-fat milk
- 2 tablespoons all-purpose flour
- 1/2 cup grated Parmesan cheese
- 1 tablespoon chopped garlic
- Salt and pepper to taste
- Fresh parsley for garnish

Directions:

1. Cook whole wheat pasta according to package instructions, aiming for al dente. Drain and set aside.
2. In a large non-stick skillet, heat olive oil over medium heat. Add chicken strips and cook until browned and no longer pink inside, about 6-8 minutes. Remove chicken from skillet and set aside.
3. In the same skillet, add garlic and sauté for 1 minute.
4. Add broccoli and sauté for another 2-3 minutes until vibrant and slightly tender.
5. Sprinkle flour over the broccoli and stir to coat. Gradually pour in low-sodium chicken broth and low-fat milk, stirring constantly.
6. Bring the mixture to a simmer and let it cook for about 5 minutes, or until the sauce has thickened.
7. Reduce heat to low and add the grated Parmesan cheese, stirring until the cheese is melted and the sauce is smooth. Season with salt and pepper to taste.
8. Return the cooked chicken to the skillet and add the cooked pasta. Toss everything together until the pasta and chicken are coated with the Alfredo sauce.
9. Serve hot, garnished with fresh parsley.

Turkey Chili with Beans

Time: 1 hour 15 minutes	Serving Size: 6
Prep Time: 15 minutes	Cook Time: 1 hour

Nutrition Information Per Serving (1 bowl):

Calories: 310, Carbohydrates: 34g, Saturated Fat: 2g, Protein: 28g, Fat: 9g, Sodium: 430mg, Potassium: 845mg, Fiber: 9g, Sugar: 6g, Vitamin C: 25%, Calcium: 8%, Iron: 20%.

Ingredients:

- 1 lb ground turkey breast
- 1 tablespoon olive oil
- 1 large onion, diced
- 3 garlic cloves, minced
- 1 red bell pepper, diced
- 1 can (15 oz) low-sodium black beans, drained and rinsed
- 1 can (15 oz) low-sodium kidney beans, drained and rinsed
- 1 can (28 oz) low-sodium diced tomatoes
- 2 tablespoons tomato paste
- 2 cups low-sodium chicken broth
- 1 tablespoon chili powder
- 1 teaspoon ground cumin
- 1 teaspoon dried oregano
- 1/2 teaspoon paprika
- Salt and pepper to taste
- Optional toppings: chopped fresh cilantro, diced avocado, low-fat sour cream

Directions:

1. Heat olive oil in a large pot over medium heat.
2. Add the ground turkey and cook until browned, breaking it apart with a spoon as it cooks.
3. Stir in onions, garlic, and red bell pepper, and cook until the vegetables are softened, about 5 minutes.
4. Mix in black beans, kidney beans, diced tomatoes, tomato paste, chicken broth, chili powder, cumin, oregano, paprika, salt, and pepper.
5. Bring the mixture to a boil, then reduce heat to low and simmer, covered, for 45 minutes, stirring occasionally.
6. Taste and adjust seasoning if necessary.
7. Serve hot with optional toppings if desired.

Baked Lemon Pepper Chicken

Time: 50 minutes	Serving Size: 4
Prep Time: 10 minutes	Cook Time: 40 minutes

Nutrition Information Per Serving (1 serving unit):

Calories: 224, Carbohydrates: 5g, Saturated Fat: 1g, Protein: 35g, Fat: 7g, Sodium: 74mg, Potassium: 370mg, Fiber: 1g, Sugar: 1g, Vitamin C: 6%, Calcium: 2%, Iron: 8%.

Ingredients:

- 4 boneless, skinless chicken breasts
- 2 lemons, one juiced and one sliced
- 1 tablespoon olive oil
- 1 tablespoon freshly ground black pepper
- 1 teaspoon sea salt
- 2 cloves garlic, minced
- 1 teaspoon dried thyme
- 1 teaspoon dried rosemary
- Fresh parsley for garnish

Directions:

1. Preheat your oven to 375°F.
2. In a small bowl, mix together the olive oil, lemon juice, black pepper, sea salt, garlic, thyme, and rosemary to create the marinade.
3. Place the chicken breasts in a baking dish and pour the marinade over them, making sure

CHAPTER 4: POULTRY DISHES

each breast is well coated.

4. Arrange the lemon slices on top of the chicken.
5. Bake in the preheated oven for 35-40 minutes or until the chicken is cooked through and reaches an internal temperature of 165°F.
6. Remove from the oven and let the chicken rest for 5 minutes before serving.
7. Garnish with fresh parsley and serve with a side of steamed vegetables or a salad for a complete meal.

Chicken Vegetable Soup

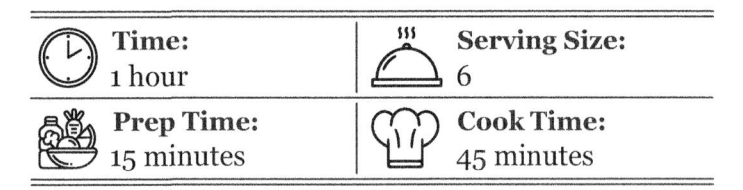

Time: 1 hour	Serving Size: 6
Prep Time: 15 minutes	Cook Time: 45 minutes

Nutrition Information Per Serving (1 bowl):

Calories: 275, Carbohydrates: 18g, Saturated Fat: 1g, Protein: 25g, Fat: 12g, Sodium: 150mg, Potassium: 600mg, Fiber: 3g, Sugar: 4g, Vitamin C: 40%, Calcium: 4%, Iron: 8%.

Ingredients:

- 1 tablespoon olive oil
- 1 large onion, chopped
- 2 garlic cloves, minced
- 2 medium carrots, sliced
- 2 celery stalks, sliced
- 1 pound boneless, skinless chicken breasts, cut into bite-sized pieces
- 6 cups low-sodium chicken broth
- 1 cup water
- 1 teaspoon dried thyme
- 1 teaspoon dried rosemary
- 1 bay leaf
- 2 cups chopped kale
- 1 cup frozen peas
- Salt and pepper to taste

Directions:

In a large pot, heat olive oil over medium heat. Add onions and garlic, sauté until onions are translucent, for about 3 minutes.

Add carrots and celery to the pot and continue to sauté for another 5 minutes.

Place the chicken pieces in the pot and cook until they are no longer pink on the outside, approximately 5 minutes.

Pour in the low-sodium chicken broth and water, and bring the mixture to a boil.

Add dried thyme, dried rosemary, and bay leaf. Reduce heat to a simmer and cover the pot. Allow to cook for 30 minutes.

Stir in the chopped kale and frozen peas, and continue to simmer for an additional 10 minutes, or until the vegetables are tender.

Remove the bay leaf, and season the soup with salt and pepper to taste before serving.

Herb Roasted Turkey Breast

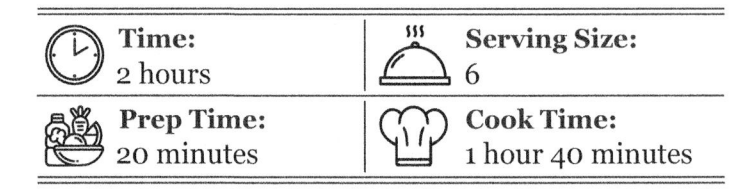

Time: 2 hours	Serving Size: 6
Prep Time: 20 minutes	Cook Time: 1 hour 40 minutes

Nutrition Information Per Serving (1 plate):

Calories: 190, Carbohydrates: 0g, Saturated Fat: 1g, Protein: 36g, Fat: 4g, Sodium: 110mg, Potassium: 20mg, Fiber: 0g, Sugar: 0g, Vitamin C: 0%, Calcium: 2%, Iron: 8%.

Ingredients:

- 1 boneless turkey breast (about 3 pounds)
- 2 tablespoons olive oil
- 4 garlic cloves, minced
- 1 tablespoon fresh rosemary, chopped
- 1 tablespoon fresh thyme, chopped
- 1 tablespoon fresh sage, chopped
- 1 teaspoon paprika
- Salt and pepper to taste

Directions:

1. Preheat your oven to 325°F.
2. In a small bowl, combine olive oil, minced garlic, rosemary, thyme, sage, paprika, salt, and pepper to create the herb mixture.
3. Place the turkey breast on a rack in a roasting pan.
4. Gently loosen the skin from the turkey breast and rub a portion of the herb mixture underneath the skin.
5. Spread the remaining herb mixture evenly over the top of the turkey breast.
6. Roast the turkey breast in the preheated oven for about 1 hour and 40 minutes, or until the internal temperature reaches 165°F when checked with a meat thermometer.
7. Remove the turkey from the oven and let it rest for 10 minutes before slicing.
8. Serve the sliced turkey breast with your choice of vegetables or a side salad for a complete meal.

Chicken Fajitas with Whole Wheat Tortillas

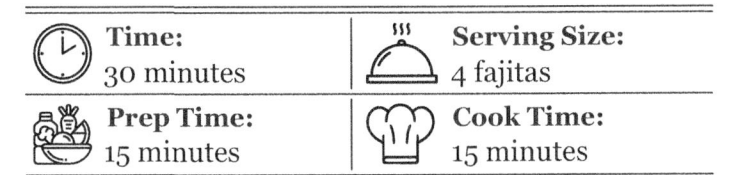

Time: 30 minutes
Serving Size: 4 fajitas
Prep Time: 15 minutes
Cook Time: 15 minutes

Nutrition Information Per Serving (1 fajita):
Calories: 350, Carbohydrates: 34g, Saturated Fat: 2g, Protein: 26g, Fat: 12g, Sodium: 320mg, Potassium: 495mg, Fiber: 5g, Sugar: 4g, Vitamin C: 125%, Calcium: 8%, Iron: 15%.

Ingredients:
- 1 lb boneless, skinless chicken breasts, thinly sliced
- 1 tablespoon canola oil
- 1 large red bell pepper, sliced
- 1 large yellow bell pepper, sliced
- 1 medium onion, sliced
- 2 cloves garlic, minced
- 1 teaspoon chili powder
- 1 teaspoon paprika
- 1 teaspoon ground cumin
- 1/2 teaspoon dried oregano
- Juice of 1 lime
- 4 whole wheat tortillas
- Salt and pepper to taste
- Fresh cilantro for garnish

Directions:

1. In a large bowl, combine the chicken slices with chili powder, paprika, ground cumin, dried oregano, salt, and pepper.
2. Heat canola oil in a large skillet over medium-high heat. Add the seasoned chicken to the skillet and sauté until browned and cooked through, about 5-6 minutes. Transfer the chicken to a plate and set aside.
3. In the same skillet, add the sliced red and yellow bell peppers, onion, and minced garlic. Cook for about 4-5 minutes or until the vegetables are tender but still crisp.
4. Return the chicken to the skillet with the vegetables and add the lime juice. Stir well to combine and cook for another 2 minutes.
5. Warm the whole wheat tortillas in the microwave or on a skillet.
6. Spoon the chicken and vegetable mixture into the center of each tortilla. Garnish with fresh cilantro.
7. Serve the fajitas with additional lime wedges on the side.

Moroccan Spiced Chicken Skewers

⏰ Time: 35 minutes	🍽 Serving Size: 4 skewers
🥗 Prep Time: 15 minutes	👨‍🍳 Cook Time: 20 minutes

Nutrition Information Per Serving (1 skewer):

Calories: 224, Carbohydrates: 5g, Saturated Fat: 0.6g, Protein: 27g, Fat: 11g, Sodium: 202mg, Potassium: 474mg, Fiber: 1.2g, Sugar: 1.4g, Vitamin C: 9%, Calcium: 3%, Iron: 10%.

Ingredients:

- 1 pound boneless, skinless chicken breasts, cut into 1-inch cubes
- 2 tablespoons olive oil
- 1 teaspoon ground cumin
- 1 teaspoon paprika
- 1/2 teaspoon ground coriander
- 1/4 teaspoon ground cinnamon
- 1/4 teaspoon cayenne pepper
- 1/4 teaspoon ground ginger
- 1/4 teaspoon ground turmeric
- 1/4 teaspoon black pepper
- 1/2 teaspoon salt
- 1 tablespoon fresh lemon juice
- 1 tablespoon fresh cilantro, chopped
- Wooden or metal skewers

Directions:

1. In a large bowl, whisk together olive oil, cumin, paprika, coriander, cinnamon, cayenne pepper, ginger, turmeric, black pepper, salt, and lemon juice to create the marinade.
2. Add the chicken cubes to the marinade and toss to coat evenly. Let the chicken marinate for at least 30 minutes in the refrigerator.
3. If using wooden skewers, soak them in water for at least 20 minutes to prevent burning. Preheat the grill to medium-high heat (around 375°F).
4. Thread the marinated chicken cubes onto the skewers, dividing them evenly.
5. Place the skewers on the grill and cook for 10 minutes on each side, or until the chicken is cooked through and has an internal temperature of 165°F.
6. Garnish the cooked chicken skewers with chopped cilantro before serving.

BBQ Pulled Chicken (with Homemade Low-Sugar Sauce)

⏰ Time: 1 hour 15 minutes	🍽 Serving Size: 4
🥗 Prep Time: 15 minutes	👨‍🍳 Cook Time: 1 hour

Nutrition Information Per Serving (1 serving unit):

Calories: 275, Carbohydrates: 10g, Saturated Fat: 1g, Protein: 35g, Fat: 8g, Sodium: 390mg, Potassium: 300mg, Fiber: 1g, Sugar: 6g, Vitamin C: 5%, Calcium: 2%, Iron: 10%.

Ingredients:

- 4 boneless, skinless chicken breasts
- 1 cup low-sodium chicken broth
- 1/2 cup tomato paste
- 2 tablespoons apple cider vinegar
- 1 tablespoon honey
- 1 tablespoon Worcestershire sauce
- 1 teaspoon garlic powder
- 1 teaspoon onion powder
- 1 teaspoon smoked paprika
- 1/2 teaspoon ground mustard
- 1/4 teaspoon cayenne pepper (optional)
- Salt and pepper to taste

Directions:

1. In a medium saucepan over medium heat, whisk together tomato paste, apple cider vinegar, honey, Worcestershire sauce, garlic

powder, onion powder, smoked paprika, ground mustard, cayenne pepper (if using), and a pinch of salt and pepper. Bring to a simmer and cook for 5 minutes, stirring frequently. Set the homemade low-sugar BBQ sauce aside.

2. Place chicken breasts in a large pot and pour in low-sodium chicken broth. Make sure the chicken is covered by the broth, adding water if necessary.

3. Bring to a boil, then reduce heat to low and simmer for about 25 minutes, or until chicken is cooked through.

4. Remove chicken from the pot and let cool slightly. Using two forks, shred the chicken into bite-sized pieces.

5. Preheat your oven to 375°F.

6. In a baking dish, combine the shredded chicken with the homemade BBQ sauce, mixing well to ensure all the chicken is coated.

7. Bake in the preheated oven for 15 minutes, until the mixture is hot and bubbly.

8. Serve the BBQ pulled chicken on whole wheat buns or over a bed of greens for a low-cholesterol meal.

Chapter 5: Vegan and Vegetarian Mains

Stuffed Bell Peppers with Lentils

Time: 1 hour		**Serving Size:** 4 peppers	
Prep Time: 20 minutes		**Cook Time:** 40 minutes	

Nutrition Information Per Serving (1 pepper):

Calories: 298, Carbohydrates: 54g, Saturated Fat: 0.5g, Protein: 14g, Fat: 3g, Sodium: 301mg, Potassium: 846mg, Fiber: 12g, Sugar: 8g, Vitamin C: 169%, Calcium: 6%, Iron: 25%.

Ingredients:

- 4 large bell peppers, tops cut off and seeds removed
- 1 cup brown lentils, rinsed and drained
- 2 cups low-sodium vegetable broth
- 1 small onion, diced
- 2 cloves garlic, minced
- 1 medium carrot, diced
- 1 celery stalk, diced
- 1 teaspoon ground cumin
- 1/2 teaspoon smoked paprika
- 1/4 teaspoon black pepper
- 1 can (14.5 oz) diced tomatoes, no salt added
- 1 cup cooked brown rice
- 2 tablespoons fresh parsley, chopped
- 1 tablespoon olive oil

Directions:

1. Preheat the oven to 350°F.
2. In a medium saucepan, combine lentils and vegetable broth. Bring to a boil, then reduce heat to low, cover, and simmer for about 20 minutes, or until lentils are tender. Drain any excess liquid.
3. While cooking the lentils, heat olive oil in a skillet over medium heat.
4. Add onion, garlic, carrot, and celery, and sauté until vegetables are softened, about 5 minutes.
5. Stir in cumin, smoked paprika, and black pepper, cooking for an additional minute until fragrant.
6. Add the cooked vegetables, diced tomatoes, and cooked brown rice to the cooked lentils. Mix well to combine.
7. Stuff each bell pepper with the lentil and rice mixture, and place them upright in a baking dish.
8. Cover with foil and bake in the preheated oven for 30-40 minutes, until the peppers are tender.
9. Garnish with fresh parsley before serving.

Vegetarian Chili

Time: 50 minutes	Serving Size: 6
Prep Time: 10 minutes	Cook Time: 40 minutes

Nutrition Information Per Serving (1 blow):

Calories: 265, Carbohydrates: 50g, Saturated Fat: 0.5g, Protein: 14g, Fat: 3g, Sodium: 300mg, Potassium: 800mg, Fiber: 13g, Sugar: 8g, Vitamin C: 40%, Calcium: 5%, Iron: 20%.

Ingredients:

- 1 tablespoon olive oil
- 1 large onion, diced
- 2 cloves garlic, minced
- 1 bell pepper, diced
- 2 carrots, peeled and diced
- 2 stalks celery, diced
- 1 zucchini, diced
- 1 yellow squash, diced
- 1 can (15 oz) low-sodium black beans, drained and rinsed
- 1 can (15 oz) low-sodium kidney beans, drained and rinsed
- 1 can (15 oz) low-sodium pinto beans, drained and rinsed
- 1 can (28 oz) low-sodium diced tomatoes
- 2 tablespoons tomato paste
- 1 tablespoon chili powder
- 1 teaspoon ground cumin
- 1 teaspoon smoked paprika
- 1/2 teaspoon dried oregano
- Salt and pepper to taste
- 2 cups vegetable broth
- Fresh cilantro, chopped (for garnish)

Directions:

1. Heat the olive oil in a large pot over medium heat. Add the onion and garlic, sautéing until the onion is translucent.
2. Stir in the bell pepper, carrots, celery, zucchini, and yellow squash, cooking until the vegetables start to soften, about 5 minutes.
3. Add the black beans, kidney beans, pinto beans, diced tomatoes, and tomato paste to the pot.
4. Season with chili powder, ground cumin, smoked paprika, dried oregano, salt, and pepper. Stir well to combine.
5. Pour in the vegetable broth and bring the mixture to a boil. Reduce heat to low and simmer for 30 minutes, stirring occasionally.
6. Taste and adjust seasoning as needed. Serve hot, garnished with fresh cilantro.

Tofu Stir-Fry with Mixed Vegetables

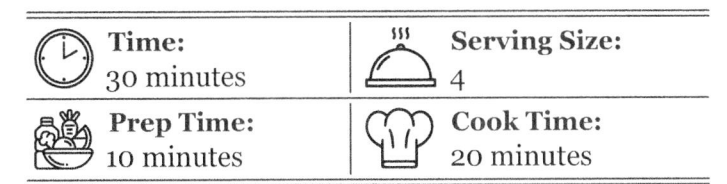

Time: 30 minutes	Serving Size: 4
Prep Time: 10 minutes	Cook Time: 20 minutes

Nutrition Information Per Serving (1 bowl):

Calories: 220, Carbohydrates: 18g, Saturated Fat: 1g, Protein: 16g, Fat: 12g, Sodium: 320mg, Potassium: 400mg, Fiber: 4g, Sugar: 6g, Vitamin C: 30%, Calcium: 15%, Iron: 19%.

Ingredients:

- 14 oz firm tofu, pressed and cut into cubes
- 1 tablespoon sesame oil
- 1 red bell pepper, sliced
- 1 yellow bell pepper, sliced
- 1 cup broccoli florets
- 1 cup snap peas
- 1 medium carrot, julienned
- 2 cloves garlic, minced
- 1 tablespoon grated ginger
- 2 tablespoons low-sodium soy sauce
- 1 tablespoon rice vinegar
- 1 teaspoon cornstarch
- 1 teaspoon maple syrup
- 1/4 cup water
- 1 tablespoon toasted sesame seeds (for garnish)
- 2 green onions, sliced (for garnish)

Directions:

CHAPTER 5: VEGAN AND VEGETARIAN MAINS

1. Wrap the tofu in a clean kitchen towel and place a heavy object on top to press out excess moisture. Leave it for at least 15 minutes. Cut the tofu into 1-inch cubes.

2. In a small bowl, whisk together the low-sodium soy sauce, rice vinegar, cornstarch, maple syrup, and water to create a stir-fry sauce. Set aside.

3. Heat sesame oil in a large skillet or wok over medium-high heat. Add the tofu cubes and stir-fry until golden brown on all sides, about 5-7 minutes. Remove tofu from the skillet and set aside.

4. In the same skillet, add the red and yellow bell peppers, broccoli, snap peas, and carrot. Stir-fry for about 3 minutes until vegetables are tender-crisp.

5. Add the minced garlic and grated ginger to the skillet and stir-fry for another minute until fragrant.

6. Return the tofu to the skillet with the vegetables. Pour the stir-fry sauce over the tofu and vegetables, stirring to coat everything evenly. Cook for an additional 2 minutes until the sauce has thickened.

7. Garnish the tofu stir-fry with toasted sesame seeds and sliced green onions.

8. Serve hot with brown rice or quinoa for a complete meal.

Vegetable Curry with Brown Rice

Time: 55 minutes
Serving Size: 4
Prep Time: 15 minutes
Cook Time: 40 minutes

Nutrition Information Per Serving (1 plate):

Calories: 330, Carbohydrates: 68g, Saturated Fat: 1g, Protein: 9g, Fat: 4g, Sodium: 480mg, Potassium: 600mg, Fiber: 9g, Sugar: 8g, Vitamin C: 80%, Calcium: 6%, Iron: 15%.

Ingredients:

- 1 cup brown rice
- 2 tablespoons olive oil
- 1 medium onion, chopped
- 2 cloves garlic, minced
- 1 tablespoon fresh ginger, grated
- 1 tablespoon curry powder
- 1 teaspoon ground turmeric
- 1/2 teaspoon cayenne pepper (optional)
- 1 medium carrot, sliced
- 1 bell pepper, chopped
- 1 cup cauliflower florets
- 1 cup green peas, frozen or fresh
- 1 can (15 oz) chickpeas, drained and rinsed
- 1 can (14.5 oz) diced tomatoes, no salt added
- 1 can (13.5 oz) coconut milk, light
- Salt to taste
- Fresh cilantro, chopped (for garnish)

Directions:

1. Cook brown rice according to package instructions; set aside.

2. Heat olive oil in a large pot over medium heat. Add onion, garlic, and ginger, and sauté until onion is translucent, about 5 minutes.

3. Stir in curry powder, turmeric, and cayenne pepper, and cook for another minute until fragrant.

4. Add carrot, bell pepper, cauliflower, and green peas to the pot. Cook for 5-7 minutes, until vegetables are slightly tender.

5. Mix in chickpeas, diced tomatoes, and coconut milk. Bring to a boil, then reduce heat to a simmer. Cook for 20 minutes, stirring occasionally.

6. Season with salt to taste. Serve the curry over the cooked brown rice and garnish with fresh cilantro.

Vegan Lentil Burgers

	Time: 45 minutes		Serving Size: 4
	Prep Time: 15 minutes		Cook Time: 30 minutes

Nutrition Information Per Serving (1 serving unit):

Calories: 320, Carbohydrates: 40g, Saturated Fat: 0.5g, Protein: 18g, Fat: 9g, Sodium: 250mg, Potassium: 550mg, Fiber: 10g, Sugar: 4g, Vitamin C: 5%, Calcium: 8%, Iron: 25%.

Ingredients:

- 1 cup dried green lentils, rinsed and drained
- 2 1/2 cups water
- 1 bay leaf
- 1/2 teaspoon salt
- 1 tablespoon olive oil
- 1 small onion, finely chopped
- 1 clove garlic, minced
- 1 carrot, grated
- 1/2 cup walnuts, finely ground
- 1/4 cup fresh parsley, chopped
- 1 tablespoon soy sauce
- 1 tablespoon tomato paste
- 1 teaspoon smoked paprika
- 1/2 teaspoon ground cumin
- 1/2 cup quick oats
- Whole grain hamburger buns
- Lettuce, tomato, and any other desired burger toppings

Directions:

1. In a medium saucepan, combine the lentils, water, bay leaf, and 1/4 teaspoon of the salt. Bring to a boil, then reduce heat and simmer uncovered for 20-25 minutes, or until lentils are tender but not mushy. Remove the bay leaf and drain any excess water.
2. While the lentils are cooking, heat the olive oil in a skillet over medium heat.
3. Add the onion and garlic, sauté until soft and translucent, for about 5 minutes.
4. Add the grated carrot and cook for another 3 minutes.
5. In a large bowl, mash half of the cooked lentils. Add the remaining whole lentils, sautéed onion, garlic, carrot, ground walnuts, parsley, soy sauce, tomato paste, smoked paprika, cumin, and the remaining 1/4 teaspoon of salt. Stir in the quick oats until well combined.
6. Preheat your oven to 375°F. Shape the lentil mixture into 4 equal-sized patties and place them on a baking sheet lined with parchment paper.
7. Bake the burgers in the preheated oven for 15 minutes, then flip them and bake for an additional 15 minutes, or until the patties are firm and lightly browned.
8. Serve the lentil burgers on whole grain buns with lettuce, tomato, and any other desired toppings.

Zucchini Lasagna (with Tofu Ricotta)

	Time: 1 hour		Serving Size: 6
	Prep Time: 20 minutes		Cook Time: 40 minutes

Nutrition Information Per Serving (1 plate):

Calories: 275, Carbohydrates: 20g, Saturated Fat: 1.5g, Protein: 19g, Fat: 13g, Sodium: 345mg, Potassium: 676mg, Fiber: 5g, Sugar: 8g, Vitamin C: 35%, Calcium: 40%, Iron: 15%.

Ingredients:

- 4 medium zucchinis, sliced lengthwise into thin strips
- 14 oz firm tofu, drained and crumbled
- 1/4 cup nutritional yeast
- 2 tablespoons lemon juice
- 1 teaspoon garlic powder
- 1 teaspoon dried basil
- 1 teaspoon dried

CHAPTER 5: VEGAN AND VEGETARIAN MAINS ◇ 41

oregano
- 1/2 teaspoon salt
- 1/4 teaspoon black pepper
- 2 cups spinach, chopped
- 2 cups marinara sauce, low-sodium
- 1/2 cup shredded vegan mozzarella cheese
- Fresh basil for garnish (optional)

Directions:

1. Preheat your oven to 375°F.
2. To make the tofu ricotta, combine the crumbled tofu, nutritional yeast, lemon juice, garlic powder, dried basil, dried oregano, salt, and black pepper in a bowl. Mix well to combine and set aside.
3. Prepare the zucchini by slicing it lengthwise into thin strips using a mandoline or sharp knife. Pat the zucchini strips dry with paper towels to remove excess moisture.
4. Spread a thin layer of marinara sauce on the bottom of a baking dish.
5. Layer zucchini strips over the sauce, then spread a layer of tofu ricotta over the zucchini. Add a layer of chopped spinach.
6. Repeat the layering process until all ingredients are used, finishing with a layer of marinara sauce. Top with shredded vegan mozzarella cheese.
7. Cover the dish with aluminum foil and bake in the preheated oven for 30 minutes.
8. Remove the foil and bake for an additional 10 minutes, or until the cheese is melted and the edges are bubbling.
9. Let the lasagna cool for 10 minutes before slicing. Garnish with fresh basil if desired and serve.

Stir-Fried Quinoa with Veggies

Time: 30 minutes	Serving Size: 4
Prep Time: 10 minutes	Cook Time: 20 minutes

Nutrition Information Per Serving (1 bowl):

Calories: 256, Carbohydrates: 45g, Saturated Fat: 0.5g, Protein: 9g, Fat: 5g, Sodium: 300mg, Potassium: 431mg, Fiber: 6g, Sugar: 4g, Vitamin C: 50%, Calcium: 4%, Iron: 15%.

Ingredients:

- 1 cup quinoa, rinsed
- 2 cups water
- 1 tablespoon olive oil
- 1 red bell pepper, diced
- 1 cup broccoli florets
- 1 medium carrot, julienned
- 1/2 cup snap peas, trimmed
- 1/2 cup red cabbage, shredded
- 2 green onions, sliced
- 2 cloves garlic, minced
- 1 tablespoon fresh ginger, minced
- 2 tablespoons low-sodium soy sauce
- 1 tablespoon sesame oil
- 1 teaspoon chili flakes (optional)
- Salt and pepper to taste
- Fresh cilantro, for garnish
- Sesame seeds, for garnish

Directions:

1. In a medium saucepan, bring 2 cups of water to a boil. Add the quinoa, reduce heat to low, cover, and simmer for 15 minutes or until all water is absorbed. Remove from heat and let stand for 5 minutes, then fluff with a fork.
2. While the quinoa is cooking, heat the olive oil in a large skillet or wok over medium-high heat. Add the red bell pepper, broccoli, carrot, and snap peas. Stir-fry for about 5 minutes until the vegetables are tender-crisp.
3. Add the red cabbage, green onions, garlic, and ginger to the skillet. Stir-fry for an

additional 2 minutes.

4. Stir in the cooked quinoa, low-sodium soy sauce, sesame oil, and chili flakes if using. Season with salt and pepper to taste. Cook for another 2 minutes, stirring frequently to combine all the ingredients well.

5. Garnish with fresh cilantro and sesame seeds before serving.

Eggplant Parmesan (Vegan Version)

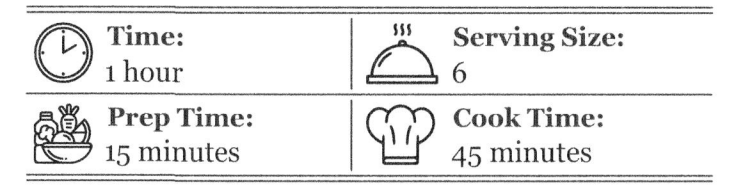

Time: 1 hour	Serving Size: 6
Prep Time: 15 minutes	Cook Time: 45 minutes

Nutrition Information Per Serving (1 serving unit):

Calories: 290, Carbohydrates: 35g, Saturated Fat: 1g, Protein: 8g, Fat: 14g, Sodium: 400mg, Potassium: 450mg, Fiber: 8g, Sugar: 10g, Vitamin C: 12%, Calcium: 5%, Iron: 10%.

Ingredients:

- 2 large eggplants, sliced into 1/2-inch rounds
- 1/4 cup olive oil
- 1/2 teaspoon salt
- 1/4 teaspoon black pepper
- 2 cups marinara sauce, low-sodium
- 1 cup vegan mozzarella cheese, shredded
- 1/2 cup vegan parmesan cheese, grated
- 1/4 cup fresh basil, chopped
- 1 tablespoon Italian seasoning
- 2 cloves garlic, minced
- Cooking spray

Directions:

1. Preheat your oven to 375°F. Spray a baking sheet with cooking spray.

2. Arrange the eggplant slices in a single layer on the prepared baking sheet. Brush each slice with olive oil and sprinkle with salt, black pepper, and Italian seasoning.

3. Bake the eggplant slices for 20 minutes, flipping halfway through until they are tender and beginning to brown.

4. In a small bowl, mix the minced garlic with the marinara sauce.

5. Spread a thin layer of the marinara sauce on the bottom of a 9x13 inch baking dish.

6. Place a layer of baked eggplant slices over the sauce. Top with more marinara sauce, then sprinkle with a portion of the vegan mozzarella and parmesan cheeses.

7. Repeat the layering process with the remaining ingredients, finishing with a layer of cheese on top.

8. Cover the dish with aluminum foil and bake for 25 minutes. Remove the foil and bake for an additional 10 minutes, or until the cheese is melted and bubbly.

9. Garnish with fresh basil before serving.

Vegan Shepherd's Pie

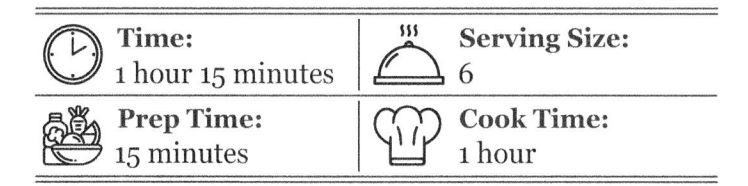

Time: 1 hour 15 minutes	Serving Size: 6
Prep Time: 15 minutes	Cook Time: 1 hour

Nutrition Information Per Serving (1 serving unit):

Calories: 330, Carbohydrates: 49g, Saturated Fat: 1g, Protein: 12g, Fat: 11g, Sodium: 400mg, Potassium: 985mg, Fiber: 11g, Sugar: 8g, Vitamin C: 25%, Calcium: 5%, Iron: 20%.

Ingredients:

- 2 lbs russet potatoes, peeled and diced
- 1/4 cup unsweetened almond milk

- 2 tablespoons vegan butter
- Salt and pepper to taste
- 1 tablespoon olive oil
- 1 large onion, diced
- 2 cloves garlic, minced
- 2 carrots, diced
- 2 celery stalks, diced
- 1 cup brown lentils, rinsed and drained
- 3 cups vegetable broth, low-sodium
- 1 teaspoon fresh thyme leaves
- 1 teaspoon fresh rosemary, chopped
- 1 cup frozen peas
- 1 cup frozen corn kernels
- 2 tablespoons tomato paste
- 1 tablespoon Worcestershire sauce, vegan
- 2 tablespoons all-purpose flour

Directions:

1. Preheat your oven to 400°F.
2. Place the diced potatoes in a large pot and cover with water. Bring to a boil, then reduce heat and simmer until potatoes are tender, about 15 minutes.
3. Drain the potatoes and return them to the pot. Add almond milk, vegan butter, and mash until smooth. Season with salt and pepper to taste. Set aside.
4. In a large skillet, heat olive oil over medium heat. Sauté onion and garlic until translucent.
5. Add carrots and celery, and cook until they begin to soften.
6. Stir in the lentils, vegetable broth, thyme, and rosemary. Bring to a boil, then reduce heat and simmer for 25 minutes, or until lentils are tender.
7. Add the frozen peas, corn, tomato paste, and vegan Worcestershire sauce. Cook for another 5 minutes.
8. Sprinkle the flour over the mixture and stir well to combine. Cook for another 2 minutes to thicken the filling.
9. Transfer the lentil mixture to a baking dish. Spread the mashed potatoes evenly on top.
10. Bake in the preheated oven for 20 minutes, or until the top is golden and the edges are bubbling.
11. Let the shepherd's pie cool for a few minutes before serving.

Mushroom Stroganoff

Time: 35 minutes	Serving Size: 4
Prep Time: 10 minutes	Cook Time: 25 minutes

Nutrition Information Per Serving (1 plate):

Calories: 280, Carbohydrates: 35g, Saturated Fat: 1g, Protein: 10g, Fat: 12g, Sodium: 320mg, Potassium: 700mg, Fiber: 6g, Sugar: 7g, Vitamin C: 5%, Calcium: 4%, Iron: 15%.

Ingredients:

- 1 pound mixed mushrooms, sliced (such as cremini, shiitake, and portobello)
- 2 tablespoons olive oil
- 1 medium onion, finely chopped
- 2 cloves garlic, minced
- 1 tablespoon all-purpose flour
- 2 cups vegetable broth, low-sodium
- 1 tablespoon soy sauce, low-sodium
- 1 teaspoon Dijon mustard
- 1/2 teaspoon smoked paprika
- 1/4 teaspoon black pepper
- 1/2 cup vegan sour cream
- 2 tablespoons fresh parsley, chopped
- Salt to taste
- Cooked whole wheat pasta or brown rice, for serving

Directions:

1. Heat the olive oil in a large skillet over

medium-high heat. Add the onions and garlic, and sauté until the onions are translucent, about 3 minutes.

2. Add the mushrooms to the skillet and cook until they release their moisture and start to brown, about 8 minutes.

3. Sprinkle the flour over the mushrooms and stir to combine. Cook for 1 minute to remove the raw flour taste.

4. Gradually pour in the vegetable broth while stirring continuously. Add the soy sauce, Dijon mustard, smoked paprika, and black pepper. Bring the mixture to a simmer and let it cook for 10 minutes, or until it thickens slightly.

5. Reduce the heat to low and stir in the vegan sour cream until well combined. Adjust the seasoning with salt if needed.

6. Serve the mushroom stroganoff over cooked whole wheat pasta or brown rice, garnished with fresh parsley.

Spaghetti Squash with Marinara Sauce

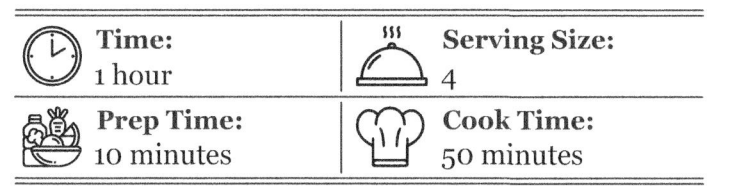

Time: 1 hour	Serving Size: 4
Prep Time: 10 minutes	Cook Time: 50 minutes

Nutrition Information Per Serving (1 plate):

Calories: 210, Carbohydrates: 30g, Saturated Fat: 0.5g, Protein: 4g, Fat: 9g, Sodium: 480mg, Potassium: 664mg, Fiber: 6g, Sugar: 12g, Vitamin C: 20%, Calcium: 5%, Iron: 8%.

Ingredients:

- 1 medium spaghetti squash (about 2 pounds)
- 2 tablespoons olive oil
- 1/4 teaspoon salt
- 1/4 teaspoon ground black pepper
- 2 cups low-sodium marinara sauce
- 1/2 cup chopped fresh basil
- 2 cloves garlic, minced
- 1 small onion, finely chopped
- 1/4 teaspoon red pepper flakes (optional)
- Vegan parmesan cheese (optional, for serving)

Directions:

1. Preheat your oven to 400°F. Cut the spaghetti squash in half lengthwise and scoop out the seeds.

2. Drizzle the inside of each half with 1 tablespoon of olive oil and season with salt and pepper. Place the squash cut-side down on a baking sheet and roast for 40 minutes, or until the flesh is easily pierced with a fork.

3. While the squash is roasting, heat the remaining olive oil in a saucepan over medium heat. Add the minced garlic, chopped onion, and red pepper flakes. Cook until the onion is translucent, about 5 minutes.

4. Pour the marinara sauce into the saucepan and bring to a simmer. Reduce heat to low and let it simmer for 10 minutes, stirring occasionally.

5. Once the squash is done, use a fork to scrape the insides and create spaghetti-like strands.

6. Serve the spaghetti squash topped with the warm marinara sauce and chopped fresh basil. If desired, sprinkle with vegan parmesan cheese before serving.

Roasted Cauliflower Tacos

Time: 30 minutes	Serving Size: 4 tacos
Prep Time: 10 minutes	Cook Time: 20 minutes

Nutrition Information Per Serving (1 taco):

Calories: 250, Carbohydrates: 35g, Saturated Fat: 2g, Protein: 8g, Fat: 10g, Sodium: 300mg, Potassium: 600mg, Fiber: 9g, Sugar: 6g, Vitamin C: 80%, Calcium: 5%, Iron: 15%.

Ingredients:

- 1 head cauliflower, cut into bite-sized florets
- 2 tablespoons olive oil
- 1 teaspoon chili powder
- 1/2 teaspoon garlic powder
- 1/2 teaspoon onion powder
- 1/4 teaspoon ground cumin
- 1/4 teaspoon paprika
- Salt and pepper to taste
- 8 corn tortillas
- 1 avocado, sliced
- 1/4 red cabbage, shredded
- 1/4 cup fresh cilantro, chopped
- 1 lime, cut into wedges
- Your favorite salsa for serving

Directions:

1. Preheat your oven to 400°F.
2. In a large bowl, toss the cauliflower florets with olive oil, chili powder, garlic powder, onion powder, cumin, paprika, salt, and pepper until well coated.
3. Spread the seasoned cauliflower on a baking sheet in a single layer and roast for 20 minutes, or until tender and slightly caramelized.
4. While the cauliflower is roasting, warm the corn tortillas in the oven for the last 5 minutes of cooking or until soft and pliable.
5. To assemble the tacos, fill each tortilla with a portion of the roasted cauliflower, avocado slices, shredded cabbage, and fresh cilantro.
6. Serve with lime wedges and your favorite salsa on the side.

Vegan Paella with Bell Peppers and Peas

Time: 55 minutes	Serving Size: 4
Prep Time: 15 minutes	Cook Time: 40 minutes

Nutrition Information Per Serving (1 bowl):

Calories: 320, Carbohydrates: 58g, Saturated Fat: 0.5g, Protein: 9g, Fat: 7g, Sodium: 400mg, Potassium: 450mg, Fiber: 6g, Sugar: 8g, Vitamin C: 80%, Calcium: 4%, Iron: 15%.

Ingredients:

- 1 cup short-grain brown rice
- 2 1/2 cups vegetable broth, low-sodium
- 1 tablespoon olive oil
- 1 large onion, diced
- 1 red bell pepper, sliced
- 1 yellow bell pepper, sliced
- 3 cloves garlic, minced
- 1 cup frozen peas
- 1 teaspoon smoked paprika
- 1/2 teaspoon turmeric
- 1/4 teaspoon cayenne pepper (optional)
- 1/2 cup tomato sauce, low-sodium
- 1 lemon, cut into wedges
- Salt and pepper to taste
- Fresh parsley, chopped for garnish

Directions:

1. In a large skillet or paella pan, heat the olive oil over medium heat. Add the onions and garlic, and sauté until the onions become translucent, about 5 minutes.
2. Stir in the red and yellow bell peppers and cook for another 3 minutes until they start to

soften.

3. Add the brown rice, smoked paprika, turmeric, and cayenne pepper to the skillet. Stir well to combine and cook for 2 minutes to toast the rice and spices together.

4. Pour in the vegetable broth and tomato sauce. Bring the mixture to a boil, then reduce the heat to low. Cover and simmer for 30 minutes, or until the rice is nearly cooked through.

5. Scatter the frozen peas over the rice, cover, and cook for an additional 10 minutes, or until the rice is tender and the peas are heated through.

6. Remove from heat and let it sit, covered, for 5 minutes. Season with salt and pepper to taste.

7. Serve the paella with lemon wedges and garnish with fresh parsley.

Chapter 6: Beef Dishes

Grilled Flank Steak with Chimichurri

Time: 35 minutes		**Serving Size:** 4	
Prep Time: 15 minutes		**Cook Time:** 20 minutes	

Nutrition Information Per Serving (1 serving unit):

Calories: 310, Carbohydrates: 5g, Saturated Fat: 4g, Protein: 24g, Fat: 20g, Sodium: 58mg, Potassium: 400mg, Fiber: 1g, Sugar: 0g, Vitamin C: 25%, Calcium: 2%, Iron: 15%.

Ingredients:

- 1 1/2 pounds flank steak
- 1/2 cup fresh parsley, finely chopped
- 1/4 cup fresh cilantro, finely chopped
- 3 cloves garlic, minced
- 2 tablespoons red wine vinegar
- 1/2 teaspoon red pepper flakes
- 1/2 cup extra virgin olive oil
- Juice of 1 lime
- Salt and pepper to taste

Directions:

1. Begin by preparing the chimichurri sauce. In a bowl, combine the parsley, cilantro, minced garlic, red wine vinegar, red pepper flakes, lime juice, and a pinch of salt and pepper. Gradually whisk in the olive oil until the sauce is well blended. Set aside to let the flavors meld.
2. Preheat the grill to high heat. While the grill is heating, take the flank steak and season both sides generously with salt and pepper.
3. Place the steak on the grill and cook for about 10 minutes on each side for medium-rare, or until it reaches your desired level of doneness.
4. Once the steak is cooked, remove it from the grill and let it rest for 5 minutes. This allows the juices to redistribute throughout the meat, ensuring it will be juicy and flavorful.
5. Slice the steak against the grain into thin strips.
6. Serve the grilled flank steak topped with the chimichurri sauce.

Beef and Broccoli Stir-Fry

Time: 25 minutes		**Serving Size:** 4	
Prep Time: 10 minutes		**Cook Time:** 15 minutes	

Nutrition Information Per Serving (1 bowl):

Calories: 275, Carbohydrates: 15g, Saturated Fat: 2g, Protein: 34g, Fat: 10g, Sodium: 350mg, Potassium: 770mg, Fiber: 3g, Sugar: 5g, Vitamin

C: 150%, Calcium: 7%, Iron: 20%.

Ingredients:

- 1 lb lean beef, thinly sliced (such as flank or sirloin)
- 4 cups broccoli florets
- 1 tablespoon olive oil
- 2 cloves garlic, minced
- 1 tablespoon fresh ginger, grated
- 1/4 cup low-sodium soy sauce
- 1 tablespoon cornstarch
- 1/2 cup low-sodium beef broth
- 1 tablespoon brown sugar
- 1 teaspoon sesame oil
- Salt and pepper to taste
- Cooked brown rice, for serving

Directions:

1. In a small bowl, whisk together the low-sodium soy sauce, cornstarch, low-sodium beef broth, brown sugar, and sesame oil. Set the mixture aside.
2. Heat the olive oil in a large skillet or wok over medium-high heat.
3. Add the minced garlic and grated ginger, then sauté for about 30 seconds until fragrant.
4. Add the thinly sliced beef to the skillet, seasoning with salt and pepper, and stir-fry until the beef is browned and cooked through, about 3-4 minutes. Remove the beef from the skillet and set aside.
5. In the same skillet, add the broccoli florets and stir-fry until they are bright green and tender-crisp, about 3 minutes.
6. Return the beef to the skillet with the broccoli.
7. Pour the sauce mixture over the beef and broccoli, and cook for another 2 minutes, stirring constantly, until the sauce has thickened.
8. Serve the beef and broccoli stir-fry over cooked brown rice.

Lean Beef Burgers with Whole Wheat Buns

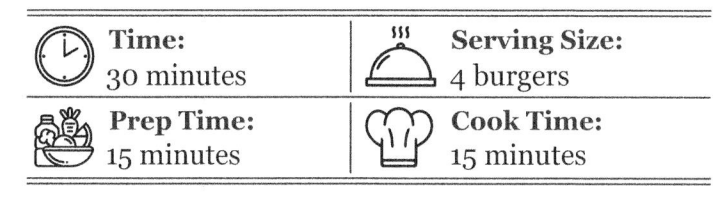

Time: 30 minutes	Serving Size: 4 burgers
Prep Time: 15 minutes	Cook Time: 15 minutes

Nutrition Information Per Serving (1 burger):

Calories: 350, Carbohydrates: 32g, Saturated Fat: 4g, Protein: 26g, Fat: 12g, Sodium: 430mg, Potassium: 350mg, Fiber: 4g, Sugar: 5g, Vitamin C: 2%, Calcium: 6%, Iron: 20%.

Ingredients:

- 1 pound lean ground beef (at least 90% lean)
- 4 whole wheat hamburger buns
- 1/2 teaspoon garlic powder
- 1/2 teaspoon onion powder
- 1/4 teaspoon ground black pepper
- 1/2 teaspoon sea salt
- 1 tablespoon Worcestershire sauce
- 4 lettuce leaves
- 1 tomato, sliced
- 1 red onion, sliced
- Mustard, ketchup, or other low-fat condiments (optional)

Directions:

1. Preheat your grill to medium-high heat (around 375°F).
2. In a bowl, mix together the lean ground beef, garlic powder, onion powder, black pepper, sea salt, and Worcestershire sauce. Form the mixture into 4 equal-sized patties.
3. Place the patties on the grill and cook for about 7-8 minutes on each side, or until the internal temperature reaches 160°F.
4. During the last few minutes of cooking, place the whole wheat buns on the grill to toast

lightly.

5. Assemble the burgers by placing a lettuce leaf on the bottom half of each bun, followed by a cooked beef patty.

6. Add a slice of tomato and red onion on top of each patty. If desired, add mustard, ketchup, or other low-fat condiments.

7. Cover with the top half of the bun and serve immediately.

Beef Stew with Root Vegetables

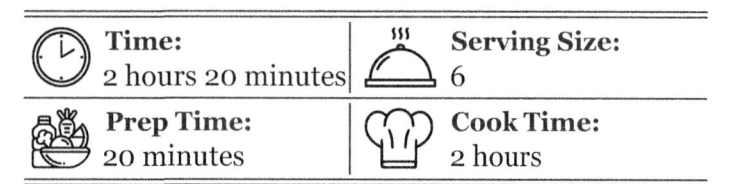

Time: 2 hours 20 minutes	Serving Size: 6
Prep Time: 20 minutes	Cook Time: 2 hours

Nutrition Information Per Serving (1 bowl):

Calories: 330, Carbohydrates: 23g, Saturated Fat: 2.5g, Protein: 35g, Fat: 10g, Sodium: 300mg, Potassium: 950mg, Fiber: 4g, Sugar: 5g, Vitamin C: 20%, Calcium: 6%, Iron: 25%.

Ingredients:

- 1 1/2 pounds lean beef chuck, cut into 1-inch cubes
- 2 tablespoons olive oil
- 3 cups low-sodium beef broth
- 1 cup water
- 2 medium carrots, peeled and sliced
- 2 parsnips, peeled and sliced
- 1 small sweet potato, peeled and cubed
- 1 onion, chopped
- 2 stalks celery, sliced
- 3 cloves garlic, minced
- 1 teaspoon dried thyme
- 1 bay leaf
- Salt and pepper to taste
- 2 tablespoons whole wheat flour (optional for thickening)
- Fresh parsley, chopped (for garnish)

Directions:

1. Heat the olive oil in a large pot over medium-high heat. Season the beef cubes with salt and pepper, then add them to the pot. Cook until browned on all sides, about 5-7 minutes.

2. Add the chopped onion and minced garlic to the pot with the beef and sauté for 2-3 minutes until the onion is translucent.

3. Sprinkle the whole wheat flour over the beef and onion mixture, and stir to coat the beef to thicken the stew.

4. Pour in the low-sodium beef broth and water, then add the carrots, parsnips, sweet potato, celery, dried thyme, and bay leaf. Bring to a boil.

5. Once boiling, reduce the heat to low, cover, and simmer for 1 hour and 45 minutes, or until the beef is tender.

6. After the stew has simmered and the beef is tender, remove the bay leaf, adjust the seasoning with salt and pepper, and serve hot.

7. Garnish with fresh parsley before serving.

Beef Lettuce Wraps

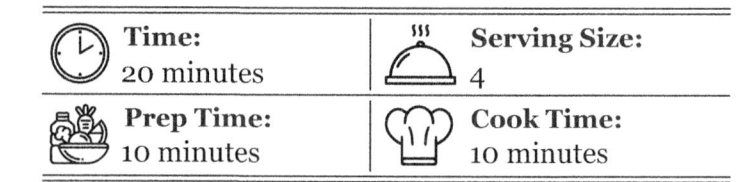

Time: 20 minutes	Serving Size: 4
Prep Time: 10 minutes	Cook Time: 10 minutes

Nutrition Information Per Serving (1 serving unit):

Calories: 220, Carbohydrates: 9g, Saturated Fat: 1.5g, Protein: 26g, Fat: 9g, Sodium: 320mg, Potassium: 440mg, Fiber: 2g, Sugar: 3g, Vitamin C: 15%, Calcium: 4%, Iron: 18%.

Ingredients:

- 1 pound lean ground beef (95% lean)
- 1 large head of butter lettuce

- 1 medium carrot, shredded
- 1 red bell pepper, thinly sliced
- 1/4 cup low-sodium soy sauce
- 2 tablespoons hoisin sauce
- 1 tablespoon rice vinegar
- 2 cloves garlic, minced
- 1 teaspoon fresh ginger, minced
- 1 teaspoon sesame oil
- 1/4 cup green onions, chopped
- 1 tablespoon sesame seeds
- Fresh cilantro leaves for garnish

Directions:

1. In a large non-stick skillet over medium heat, cook the lean ground beef with the minced garlic and ginger until the beef is browned and fully cooked, breaking it into small pieces as it cooks. Drain any excess fat if necessary.
2. In a small bowl, whisk together the low-sodium soy sauce, hoisin sauce, rice vinegar, and sesame oil to create the sauce.
3. Pour the sauce over the cooked beef in the skillet, stirring to coat the beef evenly. Cook for an additional 2 minutes to allow the flavors to meld.
4. Remove the skillet from heat and stir in the green onions and sesame seeds.
5. Carefully separate the butter lettuce leaves, rinse, and pat dry.
6. To assemble the lettuce wraps, spoon the beef mixture onto the center of a lettuce leaf, top with shredded carrot and slices of red bell pepper.
7. Garnish with fresh cilantro leaves.
8. Serve the lettuce wraps immediately, allowing diners to make their own wraps at the table.

Sirloin Steak with Grilled Vegetables

Time: 35 minutes	Serving Size: 4
Prep Time: 15 minutes	Cook Time: 20 minutes

Nutrition Information Per Serving (1 steak):

Calories: 250, Carbohydrates: 10g, Saturated Fat: 2g, Protein: 26g, Fat: 10g, Sodium: 180mg, Potassium: 610mg, Fiber: 3g, Sugar: 4g, Vitamin C: 120%, Calcium: 4%, Iron: 15%.

Ingredients:

- 4 sirloin steaks (4 ounces each), trimmed of fat
- 2 bell peppers, any color, sliced into strips
- 2 zucchinis, sliced into rounds
- 1 red onion, cut into wedges
- 2 tablespoons olive oil
- 1 teaspoon dried oregano
- 1/2 teaspoon garlic powder
- 1/2 teaspoon smoked paprika
- Salt and pepper to taste
- Fresh parsley, chopped (for garnish)

Directions:

1. Preheat the grill to medium-high heat (approximately 400°F).
2. In a large bowl, toss the bell peppers, zucchinis, and red onion with olive oil, dried oregano, garlic powder, smoked paprika, and a pinch of salt and pepper.
3. Place the vegetables on the grill and cook for about 10-12 minutes, turning occasionally until they are tender and have grill marks.
4. Season the sirloin steaks with salt and pepper to taste.
5. Place the steaks on the grill and cook for about 4-5 minutes on each side for medium-rare, or until they reach the desired level of doneness.

CHAPTER 6: BEEF DISHES

6. Remove the steaks and let them rest for a few minutes before slicing.

7. Serve the sliced sirloin steaks with the grilled vegetables and garnish with fresh parsley.

Beef Fajitas with Whole Wheat Tortillas

Time: 30 minutes	Serving Size: 4 fajitas
Prep Time: 15 minutes	Cook Time: 15 minutes

Nutrition Information Per Serving (1 fajita):

Calories: 350, Carbohydrates: 34g, Saturated Fat: 3g, Protein: 27g, Fat: 12g, Sodium: 480mg, Potassium: 500mg, Fiber: 5g, Sugar: 6g, Vitamin C: 130%, Calcium: 8%, Iron: 20%.

Ingredients:

- 1 pound lean beef flank steak
- 1 tablespoon olive oil
- 1 tablespoon lime juice
- 1 garlic clove, minced
- 1 teaspoon chili powder
- 1 teaspoon ground cumin
- 1/2 teaspoon paprika
- 1/2 teaspoon black pepper
- 1/4 teaspoon salt
- 1 onion, sliced
- 1 red bell pepper, sliced
- 1 green bell pepper, sliced
- 4 whole wheat tortillas
- 1/2 cup fresh salsa
- 1/4 cup low-fat sour cream
- 1/4 cup fresh cilantro, chopped

Directions:

1. In a bowl, mix together olive oil, lime juice, minced garlic, chili powder, ground cumin, paprika, black pepper, and salt to create the marinade.

2. Slice the beef flank steak across the grain into thin strips and place them in the marinade. Let it sit for at least 10 minutes to absorb the flavors.

3. Heat a large skillet over medium-high heat. Add the marinated beef strips and cook for about 5 minutes or until they are browned and cooked through. Remove the beef from the skillet and set aside.

4. In the same skillet, add the sliced onion and bell peppers. Sauté for about 5 minutes until the vegetables are tender-crisp.

5. Return the beef to the skillet with the vegetables and toss to combine. Cook for an additional 2 minutes.

6. Warm the whole wheat tortillas in a dry skillet or in the microwave.

7. Assemble the fajitas by spooning the beef and vegetable mixture onto the center of each tortilla.

8. Top with fresh salsa, a dollop of low-fat sour cream, and a sprinkle of chopped cilantro.

9. Fold the tortillas around the filling and serve hot.

Beef and Mushroom Skewers

Time: 45 minutes	Serving Size: 4 skewers
Prep Time: 15 minutes	Cook Time: 30 minutes

Nutrition Information Per Serving (1 skewer):

Calories: 280, Carbohydrates: 8g, Saturated Fat: 2g, Protein: 25g, Fat: 16g, Sodium: 200mg, Potassium: 650mg, Fiber: 2g, Sugar: 4g, Vitamin C: 5%, Calcium: 3%, Iron: 20%.

Ingredients:

- 1 pound sirloin steak, cut into 1-inch cubes
- 2 cups whole button mushrooms
- 1/4 cup balsamic vinegar
- 2 tablespoons olive oil
- 2 cloves garlic, minced
- 1 teaspoon dried thyme
- 1 teaspoon dried rosemary
- Salt and pepper to taste
- 8 wooden skewers, soaked in water for 30 minutes

Directions:

1. In a bowl, whisk together balsamic vinegar, olive oil, minced garlic, dried thyme, dried rosemary, and a pinch of salt and pepper to create the marinade.
2. Add the sirloin steak cubes to the marinade, toss to coat evenly, and let it marinate for at least 15 minutes, up to 2 hours in the refrigerator.
3. Preheat the grill to medium heat (around 350°F).
4. Thread the marinated steak cubes and whole button mushrooms alternately onto the soaked skewers.
5. Place the skewers on the grill and cook for about 12-15 minutes, turning occasionally, until the beef reaches the desired doneness and the mushrooms are tender.
6. Remove the skewers from the grill and let them rest for a few minutes before serving.
7. Serve the beef and mushroom skewers hot, garnished with additional fresh herbs if desired.

Slow Cooker Beef and Tomato Stew

Time: 8 hours 10 minutes	Serving Size: 6 servings
Prep Time: 15 minutes	Cook Time: 7 hours 55 minutes

Nutrition Information Per Serving (1 bowl):

Calories: 250, Carbohydrates: 15g, Saturated Fat: 2g, Protein: 35g, Fat: 7g, Sodium: 300mg, Potassium: 800mg, Fiber: 3g, Sugar: 5g, Vitamin C: 20%, Calcium: 4%, Iron: 25%.

Ingredients:

- 2 pounds lean beef chuck, cut into 1-inch cubes
- 1 tablespoon olive oil
- 3 carrots, peeled and sliced
- 2 stalks celery, chopped
- 1 large onion, chopped
- 4 cloves garlic, minced
- 1 (28 oz) can low-sodium crushed tomatoes
- 1 (6 oz) can low-sodium tomato paste
- 1/4 cup fresh basil, chopped
- 1 teaspoon dried oregano
- 1/2 teaspoon ground black pepper
- 1/2 teaspoon salt (optional)
- 2 cups low-sodium beef broth
- 1 bay leaf

Directions:

1. Heat olive oil in a skillet over medium heat. Brown the beef cubes in batches, ensuring they are just browned on all sides. Transfer the browned beef to the slow cooker.
2. Add the carrots, celery, onion, and garlic to the slow cooker with the beef.
3. In a bowl, mix together the crushed tomatoes, tomato paste, basil, oregano, black pepper, and salt if using. Pour this mixture over the beef and vegetables in the slow cooker.
4. Pour in the low-sodium beef broth and add the bay leaf.

5. Cover and cook on low for 7-8 hours, until the beef is tender.

6. Remove the bay leaf before serving. Serve hot, garnished with additional fresh basil if desired.

Beef and Barley Soup

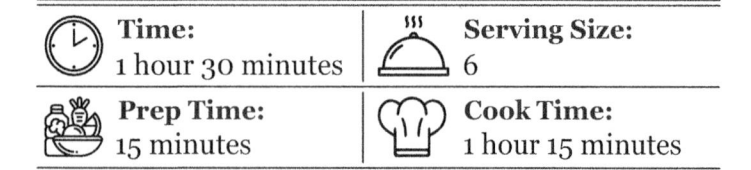

⏰ Time: 1 hour 30 minutes	🍽 Serving Size: 6
🥗 Prep Time: 15 minutes	👨‍🍳 Cook Time: 1 hour 15 minutes

Nutrition Information Per Serving (1 bowl):

Calories: 256, Carbohydrates: 20g, Saturated Fat: 2g, Protein: 17g, Fat: 10g, Sodium: 300mg, Potassium: 370mg, Fiber: 4g, Sugar: 2g, Vitamin C: 12%, Calcium: 2%, Iron: 15%.

Ingredients:

- 1 pound lean beef stew meat, trimmed and cubed
- 1 tablespoon olive oil
- 1 large onion, chopped
- 2 carrots, peeled and sliced
- 2 celery stalks, sliced
- 2 garlic cloves, minced
- 3/4 cup pearl barley, rinsed
- 6 cups low-sodium beef broth
- 1 bay leaf
- 1/2 teaspoon dried thyme
- Salt and pepper to taste
- 1/4 cup fresh parsley, chopped
- 1 tablespoon tomato paste

Directions:

1. In a large pot, heat olive oil over medium-high heat. Add the beef cubes and cook until browned on all sides.

2. Add the chopped onion, sliced carrots, and celery to the pot with the beef. Cook for about 5 minutes, until the vegetables start to soften.

3. Stir in the minced garlic and cook for another minute until fragrant.

4. Add the rinsed barley, low-sodium beef broth, bay leaf, dried thyme, and tomato paste to the pot. Season with salt and pepper to taste.

5. Bring the soup to a boil, then reduce the heat to low, cover, and simmer for about 1 hour, or until the barley and beef are tender.

6. Remove the bay leaf, adjust seasoning if necessary, and stir in the chopped fresh parsley just before serving.

Lean Meatloaf with Oats

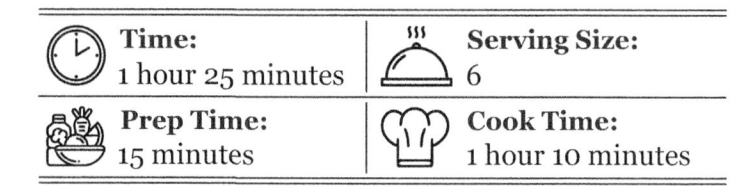

⏰ Time: 1 hour 25 minutes	🍽 Serving Size: 6
🥗 Prep Time: 15 minutes	👨‍🍳 Cook Time: 1 hour 10 minutes

Nutrition Information Per Serving (1 serving unit):

Calories: 350, Carbohydrates: 14g, Saturated Fat: 3g, Protein: 26g, Fat: 20g, Sodium: 480mg, Potassium: 370mg, Fiber: 2g, Sugar: 5g, Vitamin C: 1%, Calcium: 4%, Iron: 15%.

Ingredients:

- 1 1/2 pounds lean ground beef (90% lean)
- 1 cup rolled oats
- 1/2 cup low-fat milk
- 1/2 cup tomato sauce, low-sodium
- 1 small onion, finely chopped
- 1 carrot, shredded
- 2 cloves garlic, minced
- 1 large egg, beaten
- 2 tablespoons Worcestershire sauce
- 1 teaspoon dried thyme
- 1 teaspoon dried parsley
- 1/2 teaspoon black pepper
- 1/4 teaspoon salt (optional)

Directions:

1. Preheat the oven to 350°F.

2. In a large bowl, combine the lean ground beef, rolled oats, and low-fat milk. Let the mixture sit for 5 minutes to allow the oats to absorb the milk.

3. Add the tomato sauce, chopped onion, shredded carrot, minced garlic, beaten egg, Worcestershire sauce, dried thyme, dried parsley, black pepper, and salt to the beef and oats mixture. Mix until well combined.

4. Transfer the mixture to a loaf pan that has been lightly greased or lined with parchment paper.

5. Shape the mixture into a loaf within the pan.

6. Bake in the preheated oven for about 70 minutes, or until the meatloaf is cooked through and a meat thermometer inserted into the center reads 160°F.

7. Let the meatloaf rest for 10 minutes before slicing and serving.

Beef and Spinach Stuffed Peppers

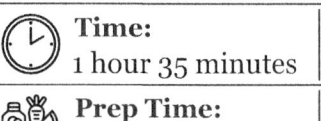

Time: 1 hour 35 minutes	Serving Size: 4 pepper
Prep Time: 20 minutes	Cook Time: 1 hour 15 minutes

Nutrition Information Per Serving (1 stuffed pepper):

Calories: 289, Carbohydrates: 18g, Saturated Fat: 2.5g, Protein: 27g, Fat: 12g, Sodium: 321mg, Potassium: 674mg, Fiber: 4g, Sugar: 6g, Vitamin C: 190%, Calcium: 6%, Iron: 22%.

Ingredients:

- 4 large bell peppers, tops cut, stemmed and seeded
- 1/2 pound extra-lean ground beef
- 1 cup cooked brown rice
- 1 cup fresh spinach, chopped
- 1/2 cup onion, finely chopped
- 2 cloves garlic, minced
- 1 (14.5 oz) can no-salt-added diced tomatoes, drained
- 1 teaspoon dried oregano
- 1/2 teaspoon dried basil
- 1/4 teaspoon salt
- 1/4 teaspoon black pepper
- 1/2 cup reduced-fat shredded mozzarella cheese
- 1/2 cup low-sodium vegetable broth

Directions:

1. Preheat your oven to 350°F.

2. In a skillet over medium heat, cook the ground beef with onions and garlic until the beef is browned and the onions are tender.

3. Drain any excess fat. Stir in the spinach and cook until wilted.

4. Add the cooked brown rice, diced tomatoes, oregano, basil, salt, and pepper to the skillet and mix well.

5. Cook for an additional 3 minutes, then remove from heat.

6. Stuff each bell pepper with the beef and rice mixture and place them in a baking dish. Pour the vegetable broth into the bottom of the dish.

7. Cover with foil and bake for 35 minutes.

8. Uncover, top each pepper with shredded mozzarella cheese, and bake for an additional 10 minutes or until the cheese is melted and bubbly. Serve warm.

Balsamic Marinated Roast Beef

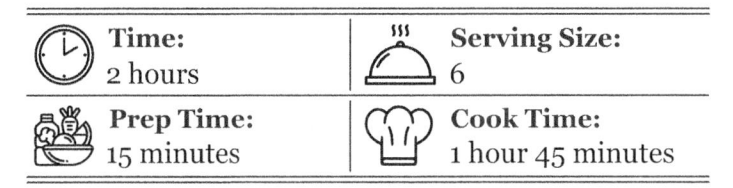

Time: 2 hours	Serving Size: 6
Prep Time: 15 minutes	Cook Time: 1 hour 45 minutes

Nutrition Information Per Serving (1 serving unit):

Calories: 210, Carbohydrates: 5g, Saturated Fat: 2g, Protein: 34g, Fat: 7g, Sodium: 320mg, Potassium: 500mg, Fiber: 0g, Sugar: 4g, Vitamin C: 1%, Calcium: 3%, Iron: 25%.

Ingredients:

- 2 pounds beef round roast, trimmed of visible fat
- 1/4 cup balsamic vinegar
- 2 tablespoons olive oil
- 3 garlic cloves, minced
- 2 teaspoons dried rosemary
- 1 teaspoon dried thyme
- 1/2 teaspoon black pepper
- 1/4 teaspoon salt (optional)
- 1/2 cup low-sodium beef broth

Directions:

1. In a small bowl, whisk together balsamic vinegar, olive oil, minced garlic, rosemary, thyme, black pepper, and salt (if using) to create the marinade.
2. Place the beef round roast in a large resealable plastic bag and pour the marinade over the beef. Seal the bag and ensure the beef is well-coated with the marinade. Refrigerate for at least 2 hours, or overnight for better flavor.
3. Preheat the oven to 325°F.
4. Remove the beef from the marinade and place it in a roasting pan. Pour the low-sodium beef broth around the beef in the pan.
5. Roast in the preheated oven for about 1 hour and 45 minutes, or until the desired doneness is reached. For medium-rare, a meat thermometer should read 145°F when inserted into the thickest part of the roast.
6. Once cooked, remove the roast from the oven and let it rest for 10-15 minutes before slicing. This allows the juices to redistribute throughout the meat.
7. Slice the roast beef thinly against the grain and serve.

Chapter 7: Fish and Seafood

Grilled Salmon with Lemon and Dill

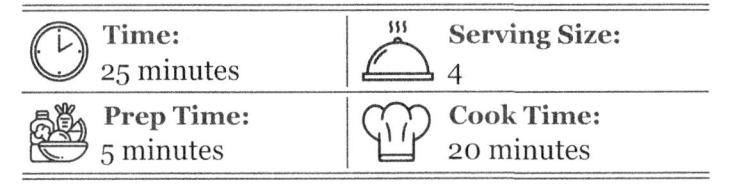

Time: 25 minutes	Serving Size: 4
Prep Time: 5 minutes	Cook Time: 20 minutes

Time: 25 minutes

Serving Size: 4

Prep Time: 5 minutes

Cook Time: 20 minutes

Nutrition Information Per Serving (1 fillet):

Calories: 230, Carbohydrates: 1g, Saturated Fat: 1g, Protein: 25g, Fat: 14g, Sodium: 50mg, Potassium: 500mg, Fiber: 0g, Sugar: 0g, Vitamin C: 8%, Calcium: 2%, Iron: 6%.

Ingredients:

- 4 salmon fillets (6 ounces each), skin on
- 2 tablespoons fresh dill, chopped
- 1 lemon, thinly sliced
- 1 tablespoon olive oil
- 1/4 teaspoon black pepper
- 1/4 teaspoon garlic powder
- Lemon wedges, for serving

Directions:

1. Preheat the grill to medium-high heat (around 375°F).
2. Rinse the salmon fillets and pat them dry with paper towels.
3. Brush each fillet with olive oil and season with black pepper and garlic powder.
4. Sprinkle the chopped dill evenly over the fillets and arrange lemon slices on top.
5. Place the salmon fillets, skin side down, on the grill.
6. Grill the salmon for about 15-20 minutes, or until the fish flakes easily with a fork and the internal temperature reaches 145°F.
7. Carefully remove the salmon from the grill and serve immediately with additional lemon wedges.

Baked Cod with Tomato and Basil

Time: 30 minutes	Serving Size: 4
Prep Time: 10 minutes	Cook Time: 20 minutes

Nutrition Information Per Serving (1 serving unit):

Calories: 189, Carbohydrates: 5g, Saturated Fat: 0.4g, Protein: 28g, Fat: 7g, Sodium: 87mg, Potassium: 670mg, Fiber: 1g, Sugar: 2g, Vitamin C: 25%, Calcium: 4%, Iron: 5%.

Ingredients:

- 4 cod fillets (6 ounces each)
- 2 medium tomatoes, sliced

- 1/4 cup fresh basil leaves, chopped
- 2 tablespoons extra virgin olive oil
- 2 cloves garlic, minced
- 1 lemon, zest and juice
- Salt and pepper to taste
- Fresh basil leaves for garnish

Directions:

1. Preheat your oven to 400°F.
2. Place the cod fillets in a baking dish coated with a thin layer of olive oil.
3. Season the fillets with salt and pepper to taste.
4. In a small bowl, combine the minced garlic, lemon zest, and lemon juice.
5. Spoon this mixture over the cod fillets. Arrange the tomato slices on top of each fillet and sprinkle with chopped basil.
6. Drizzle the remaining olive oil over the tomatoes.
7. Bake in the preheated oven for 20 minutes, or until the fish flakes easily with a fork.
8. Garnish with fresh basil leaves before serving.
9. Enjoy this heart-healthy dish with a side of steamed vegetables or a green salad for a complete meal.

Shrimp Stir-Fry with Vegetables

Time: 30 minutes
Serving Size: 4
Prep Time: 10 minutes
Cook Time: 20 minutes

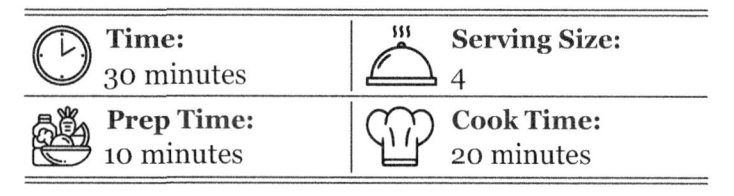

Nutrition Information Per Serving (1 serving unit):

Calories: 220, Carbohydrates: 12g, Saturated Fat: 0.5g, Protein: 25g, Fat: 8g, Sodium: 330mg, Potassium: 340mg, Fiber: 3g, Sugar: 5g, Vitamin C: 25%, Calcium: 18%, Iron: 15%.

Ingredients:

- 1 pound large shrimp, peeled and deveined
- 2 tablespoons olive oil
- 1 red bell pepper, sliced into strips
- 1 yellow bell pepper, sliced into strips
- 1 medium zucchini, sliced into half-moons
- 1 cup snap peas
- 1 medium carrot, julienned
- 2 cloves garlic, minced
- 1 tablespoon fresh ginger, minced
- 2 tablespoons low-sodium soy sauce
- 1 tablespoon rice vinegar
- 1 teaspoon sesame oil
- 1 teaspoon honey
- 1/4 teaspoon crushed red pepper flakes (optional)
- 2 green onions, sliced for garnish
- 1 tablespoon sesame seeds for garnish

Directions:

1. In a large wok or skillet, heat 1 tablespoon of olive oil over medium-high heat. Add the shrimp and stir-fry until they turn pink and are cooked through, about 3-4 minutes. Remove the shrimp from the wok and set aside.
2. Add the remaining tablespoon of olive oil to the wok. Stir-fry the red and yellow bell peppers, zucchini, snap peas, and carrot until they are tender-crisp, about 5 minutes.
3. Add the minced garlic and ginger to the vegetables and stir-fry for an additional minute.
4. In a small bowl, whisk together the low-sodium soy sauce, rice vinegar, sesame oil, honey, and red pepper flakes. Pour this sauce over the vegetables in the wok.
5. Return the cooked shrimp to the wok and toss to combine with the vegetables and sauce.

Cook for another 1-2 minutes until everything is heated through.

6. Garnish with sliced green onions and sesame seeds before serving.

Seafood Paella (with Brown Rice)

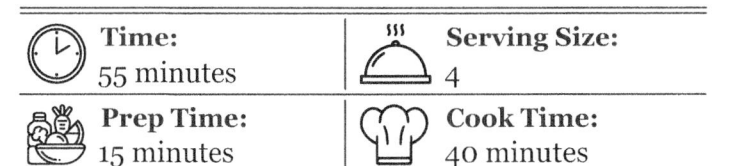

Time: 55 minutes	Serving Size: 4
Prep Time: 15 minutes	Cook Time: 40 minutes

Nutrition Information Per Serving (1 bowl):

Calories: 380, Carbohydrates: 45g, Saturated Fat: 1g, Protein: 25g, Fat: 10g, Sodium: 300mg, Potassium: 400mg, Fiber: 4g, Sugar: 3g, Vitamin C: 25%, Calcium: 6%, Iron: 15%.

Ingredients:

- 1 cup brown rice
- 2 cups low-sodium chicken broth
- 1/2 pound shrimp, peeled and deveined
- 1/2 pound mussels, cleaned and debearded
- 1/2 pound scallops
- 1 medium onion, chopped
- 3 cloves garlic, minced
- 1 red bell pepper, sliced
- 1/2 cup frozen peas
- 1/4 cup fresh parsley, chopped
- 1 teaspoon smoked paprika
- 1/2 teaspoon saffron threads
- 2 tablespoons olive oil
- Salt and pepper to taste
- Lemon wedges for serving

Directions:

1. Preheat the oven to 375°F.
2. In a large ovenproof skillet or paella pan, heat the olive oil over medium heat.
3. Add the onion and garlic, sautéing until the onion is translucent.
4. Stir in the red bell pepper and cook for another 2 minutes.
5. Add the brown rice, smoked paprika, saffron, salt, and pepper, stirring to combine.
6. Pour in the low-sodium chicken broth and bring the mixture to a simmer.
7. Cover the skillet with a lid or aluminum foil and place it in the oven.
8. Bake for 30 minutes or until the rice is almost tender.
9. Remove the skillet from the oven and stir in the shrimp, mussels, scallops, and peas.
10. Cover and bake for an additional 10 minutes or until the seafood is cooked through and the mussels have opened. Discard any unopened mussels.
11. Garnish with fresh parsley and serve with lemon wedges on the side.

Tuna Salad Stuffed Avocado

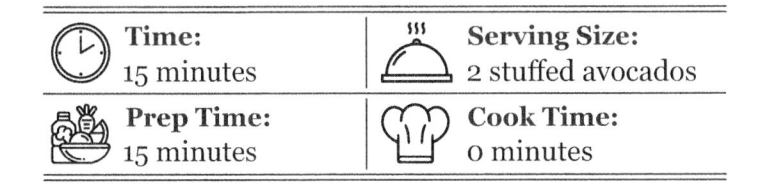

Time: 15 minutes	Serving Size: 2 stuffed avocados
Prep Time: 15 minutes	Cook Time: 0 minutes

Nutrition Information Per Serving (1 stuffed avocado):

Calories: 250, Carbohydrates: 10g, Saturated Fat: 1.5g, Protein: 15g, Fat: 18g, Sodium: 300mg, Potassium: 600mg, Fiber: 7g, Sugar: 1g, Vitamin C: 20mg, Calcium: 30mg, Iron: 1.5mg.

Ingredients:

- 1 can (5 ounces) tuna in water, drained
- 2 ripe avocados, halved and pitted
- 1/4 cup diced red onion
- 1/4 cup diced cucumber
- 1/4 cup cherry tomatoes, halved
- 2 tablespoons light mayonnaise

- 1 tablespoon Dijon mustard
- 1 tablespoon fresh lemon juice
- Salt and pepper to taste
- Fresh parsley for garnish

Directions:

1. In a medium bowl, combine drained tuna, diced red onion, diced cucumber, cherry tomatoes, light mayonnaise, Dijon mustard, and fresh lemon juice. Mix well until all ingredients are evenly incorporated.
2. Cut a small portion from the bottom of each avocado half to create a stable base.
3. Scoop out some of the avocado flesh, leaving a well in the center for the tuna salad. Dice the scooped avocado and add it to the tuna mixture for added creaminess.
4. Gently fold the tuna salad mixture until the diced avocado is evenly distributed.
5. Season the tuna salad with salt and pepper to taste.
6. Spoon the tuna salad into each avocado half, creating a generous mound on top.
7. Garnish with fresh parsley for a burst of color and added freshness.
8. Serve the Tuna Salad Stuffed Avocado immediately as a light and satisfying meal.

Fish Tacos with Cabbage Slaw

Time: 30 minutes
Serving Size: 4 tacos
Prep Time: 15 minutes
Cook Time: 15 minutes

Nutrition Information Per Serving (1 taco):

Calories: 280, Carbohydrates: 25g, Saturated Fat: 1.5g, Protein: 20g, Fat: 10g, Sodium: 350mg, Potassium: 450mg, Fiber: 4g, Sugar: 3g, Vitamin C: 30mg, Calcium: 80mg, Iron: 2mg.

Ingredients:

- 1 pound white fish fillets (such as tilapia or cod)
- 2 tablespoons olive oil
- 1 teaspoon ground cumin
- 1 teaspoon smoked paprika
- 1/2 teaspoon garlic powder
- Salt and pepper to taste
- 8 small whole wheat or corn tortillas

For Cabbage Slaw:

- 2 cups shredded green cabbage
- 1/2 cup shredded carrot
- 1/4 cup chopped fresh cilantro
- 2 tablespoons plain Greek yogurt
- 1 tablespoon mayonnaise
- 1 tablespoon fresh lime juice
- Salt and pepper to taste

For Garnish:

- Sliced avocado
- Fresh lime wedges
- Hot sauce (optional)

Directions:

1. Preheat the oven to 400°F.
2. In a small bowl, mix together olive oil, ground cumin, smoked paprika, garlic powder, salt, and pepper to create a spice rub.
3. Rub the spice mixture evenly over the fish fillets.
4. Place the seasoned fish fillets on a baking sheet lined with parchment paper and bake for 12-15 minutes or until the fish is cooked through and flakes easily.
5. While the fish is baking, prepare the cabbage slaw. In a large bowl, combine shredded green cabbage, shredded carrot, chopped cilantro, Greek yogurt, mayonnaise, fresh lime juice, salt, and pepper. Toss until well coated.

6. Heat the tortillas according to package instructions.
7. Once the fish is done, flake it into bite-sized pieces.
8. Assemble the fish tacos by placing a generous amount of flaked fish onto each tortilla, topped with a scoop of cabbage slaw.
9. Garnish with sliced avocado, fresh lime wedges, and hot sauce if desired.
10. Serve the Fish Tacos with Cabbage Slaw immediately, savoring the flavors of this heart-healthy and delicious dish.

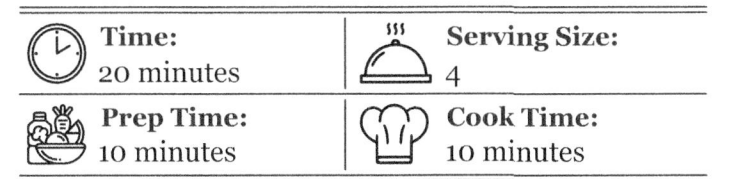

Mussels in White Wine and Garlic Sauce

Time: 20 minutes	Serving Size: 4
Prep Time: 10 minutes	Cook Time: 10 minutes

Nutrition Information Per Serving (1 serving unit):

Calories: 180, Carbohydrates: 10g, Saturated Fat: 1g, Protein: 15g, Fat: 8g, Sodium: 350mg, Potassium: 300mg, Fiber: 1g, Sugar: 1g, Vitamin C: 20mg, Calcium: 40mg, Iron: 5mg.

Ingredients:

- 2 pounds fresh mussels, cleaned and debearded
- 2 tablespoons olive oil
- 4 cloves garlic, minced
- 1/2 cup white wine
- 1 cup low-sodium chicken broth
- 2 tablespoons fresh parsley, chopped
- Salt and pepper to taste
- Crushed red pepper flakes (optional, for added heat)
- 1 lemon, cut into wedges

Directions:

1. Rinse the fresh mussels under cold water and scrub them to remove any debris. Discard any open or cracked mussels.
2. In a large pot over medium heat, heat olive oil. Add minced garlic and sauté for 1-2 minutes until fragrant.
3. Pour in the white wine, chicken broth, and add fresh parsley. Season with salt, pepper, and optional crushed red pepper flakes for added heat.
4. Bring the liquid to a simmer, then add the cleaned mussels to the pot. Cover with a lid and cook for 5-7 minutes, shaking the pot occasionally.
5. Discard any mussels that remain closed after cooking.
6. Once the mussels are cooked, transfer them to a serving bowl, pouring the flavorful broth over them.
7. Garnish with additional fresh parsley and immediately serve the Mussels in White Wine and Garlic Sauce.
8. Provide lemon wedges on the side for a citrusy burst of flavor.

Baked Tilapia with Roasted Vegetables

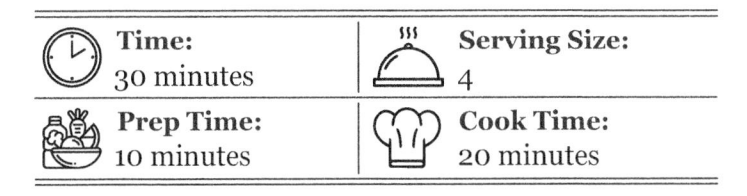

Time: 30 minutes	Serving Size: 4
Prep Time: 10 minutes	Cook Time: 20 minutes

Nutrition Information Per Serving (1 serving unit):

Calories: 250, Carbohydrates: 15g, Saturated Fat: 1g, Protein: 25g, Fat: 10g, Sodium: 350mg, Potassium: 600mg, Fiber: 4g, Sugar: 5g, Vitamin

C: 30mg, Calcium: 40mg, Iron: 2mg.

Ingredients:

- 4 Tilapia fillets
- 1 pound cherry tomatoes, halved
- 1 zucchini, sliced
- 1 yellow bell pepper, sliced
- 1 red onion, sliced
- 3 cloves garlic, minced
- 2 tablespoons olive oil
- 1 teaspoon dried oregano
- 1 teaspoon dried thyme
- Salt and pepper to taste
- Fresh parsley for garnish

Directions:

1. Preheat the oven to 400°F.
2. Place the tilapia fillets on a baking sheet lined with parchment paper. Season both sides with salt, pepper, and a pinch of dried thyme.
3. In a large bowl, combine the halved cherry tomatoes, sliced zucchini, yellow bell pepper, red onion, and minced garlic.
4. Drizzle the olive oil over the vegetables and toss to coat evenly. Season the vegetables with dried oregano, salt, and pepper. Mix well.
5. Spread the seasoned vegetables around the tilapia fillets on the baking sheet.
6. Bake in the preheated oven for 20 minutes or until the tilapia is cooked through and flakes easily with a fork.
7. Garnish with fresh parsley before serving.
8. Serve the Baked Tilapia with Roasted Vegetables hot, and enjoy a flavorful, heart-healthy meal that's low in cholesterol.

Crab Cakes with Yogurt Dill Sauce

Time: 35 minutes	Serving Size: 4 crab cakes
Prep Time: 15 minutes	Cook Time: 20 minutes

Nutrition Information Per Serving (1 crab cake):

Calories: 180, Carbohydrates: 10g, Saturated Fat: 1g, Protein: 18g, Fat: 8g, Sodium: 350mg, Potassium: 250mg, Fiber: 1g, Sugar: 2g, Vitamin C: 15mg, Calcium: 60mg, Iron: 2mg.

Ingredients:

- 1 pound lump crab meat, picked over for shells
- 1/2 cup whole wheat breadcrumbs
- 1/4 cup light mayonnaise
- 1 tablespoon Dijon mustard
- 1 tablespoon Worcestershire sauce
- 1 green onion, finely chopped
- 1 egg, beaten
- 2 tablespoons fresh parsley, chopped
- 1 teaspoon Old Bay seasoning
- Salt and pepper to taste
- 2 tablespoons olive oil
- For Yogurt Dill Sauce:
- 1/2 cup Greek yogurt
- 1 tablespoon fresh dill, chopped
- 1 tablespoon lemon juice
- Salt and pepper to taste

Directions:

1. In a large bowl, combine the lump crab meat, whole wheat breadcrumbs, light mayonnaise, Dijon mustard, Worcestershire sauce, green onion, beaten egg, fresh parsley, Old Bay seasoning, salt, and pepper. Gently fold the ingredients together until well combined.
2. Form the crab mixture into 8 equal-sized patties and place them on a plate.
3. In a skillet, heat olive oil over medium heat. Once hot, add the crab cakes and cook for 3-4 minutes per side or until golden brown and

heated through.

4. While the crab cakes are cooking, prepare the Yogurt Dill Sauce. In a small bowl, mix together Greek yogurt, fresh dill, lemon juice, salt, and pepper. Adjust the seasoning to taste.

5. Serve the Crab Cakes with a dollop of Yogurt Dill Sauce on top.

6. Garnish with additional fresh dill and lemon wedges if desired.

7. Enjoy these delicious and heart-healthy crab cakes that are low in cholesterol and bursting with flavor.

Clam Chowder (Lightened Version)

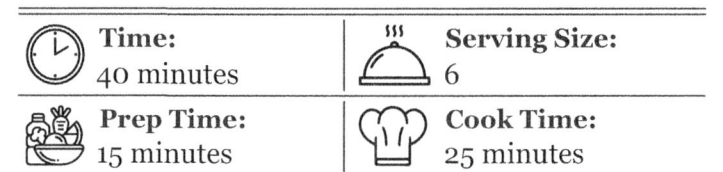

Time: 40 minutes	Serving Size: 6
Prep Time: 15 minutes	Cook Time: 25 minutes

Nutrition Information Per Serving (1 bowl):

Calories: 220, Carbohydrates: 20g, Saturated Fat: 1.5g, Protein: 12g, Fat: 10g, Sodium: 350mg, Potassium: 400mg, Fiber: 2g, Sugar: 3g, Vitamin C: 20mg, Calcium: 120mg, Iron: 2mg.

Ingredients:

- 2 slices turkey bacon, chopped
- 1 medium onion, finely diced
- 2 celery stalks, finely diced
- 2 cloves garlic, minced
- 3 cups low-sodium chicken broth
- 1 bay leaf
- 3 cups diced potatoes
- 2 cups chopped cauliflower
- 2 cups chopped clams, drained
- 2 cups 2% milk
- 1/2 cup corn kernels (fresh or frozen)
- 2 tablespoons all-purpose flour
- Salt and pepper to taste
- Chopped fresh parsley for garnish

Directions:

1. In a large pot over medium heat, cook the chopped turkey bacon until it becomes crispy. Remove excess fat, leaving about a tablespoon in the pot.

2. Add the finely diced onion, celery, and minced garlic to the pot. Sauté until the vegetables are softened, about 5 minutes.

3. Pour in the low-sodium chicken broth and add the bay leaf, diced potatoes, and chopped cauliflower. Bring the mixture to a boil, then reduce heat and simmer until the potatoes are tender, approximately 15 minutes.

4. In a separate bowl, whisk together the 2% milk and all-purpose flour until smooth. Gradually add this mixture to the pot, stirring continuously to avoid lumps.

5. Stir in the chopped clams and corn kernels. Continue to simmer for an additional 5-7 minutes, allowing the chowder to thicken.

6. Season the clam chowder with salt and pepper to taste. Discard the bay leaf.

7. Ladle the chowder into bowls, and garnish with chopped fresh parsley.

8. Serve this lightened version of Clam Chowder hot, savoring the rich flavors without compromising on heart health.

Grilled Scallops with Lemon Butter Sauce

Time: 20 minutes	Serving Size: 4
Prep Time: 10 minutes	Cook Time: 10 minutes

Nutrition Information Per Serving (1

serving unit):

Calories: 180, Carbohydrates: 3g, Saturated Fat: 2g, Protein: 20g, Fat: 10g, Sodium: 300mg, Potassium: 250mg, Fiber: 0g, Sugar: 0g, Vitamin C: 15mg, Calcium: 20mg, Iron: 1mg.

Ingredients:

- 1 pound fresh scallops, patted dry
- 2 tablespoons olive oil
- Salt and pepper to taste
- 1/4 cup unsalted butter
- 3 cloves garlic, minced
- Zest of 1 lemon
- 2 tablespoons lemon juice
- 2 tablespoons fresh parsley, chopped

Directions:

1. Preheat the grill to medium-high heat (about 400°F).
2. In a bowl, toss the fresh scallops with olive oil, salt, and pepper until evenly coated.
3. Thread the scallops onto skewers, ensuring they are spaced apart for even cooking.
4. Place the skewers on the preheated grill and cook for 4-5 minutes per side, or until the scallops are opaque and have grill marks.
5. While the scallops are grilling, prepare the lemon butter sauce. In a small saucepan over medium heat, melt the unsalted butter.
6. Add the minced garlic to the melted butter and sauté for 1-2 minutes until fragrant.
7. Remove the saucepan from heat and stir in the lemon zest and lemon juice. Mix well.
8. Once the scallops are done grilling, transfer them to a serving platter and drizzle with the lemon butter sauce.
9. Garnish with chopped fresh parsley for a burst of color and flavor.
10. Serve the Grilled Scallops with Lemon Butter Sauce immediately, and savor the delightful combination of perfectly grilled scallops and zesty lemon butter.

Salmon Patties with Whole Wheat Breadcrumbs

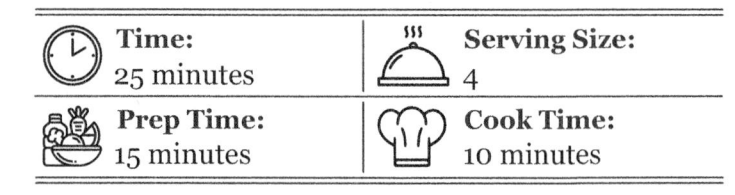

Time: 25 minutes	Serving Size: 4
Prep Time: 15 minutes	Cook Time: 10 minutes

Nutrition Information Per Serving (1 serving unit):

Calories: 220, Carbohydrates: 15g, Saturated Fat: 1.5g, Protein: 20g, Fat: 10g, Sodium: 300mg, Potassium: 350mg, Fiber: 3g, Sugar: 2g, Vitamin C: 10mg, Calcium: 40mg, Iron: 2mg.

Ingredients:

- 2 cans (14 ounces each) pink salmon, drained and flaked
- 1/2 cup whole wheat breadcrumbs
- 1/4 cup finely chopped red onion
- 1/4 cup finely chopped celery
- 2 tablespoons light mayonnaise
- 1 tablespoon Dijon mustard
- 1 tablespoon fresh lemon juice
- 1 teaspoon Old Bay seasoning
- 1/2 teaspoon garlic powder
- Salt and pepper to taste
- 2 tablespoons olive oil for cooking

Directions:

1. In a large mixing bowl, combine the flaked salmon, whole wheat breadcrumbs, chopped red onion, chopped celery, light mayonnaise, Dijon mustard, fresh lemon juice, Old Bay seasoning, garlic powder, salt, and pepper. Mix until well combined.
2. Divide the mixture into 4 equal portions and shape each portion into a patty.

3. Heat olive oil in a skillet over medium heat.

4. Carefully place the salmon patties in the skillet and cook for 4-5 minutes on each side or until they are golden brown and cooked through.

5. Remove the salmon patties from the skillet and place them on a serving platter.

6. Serve the Salmon Patties with a side of steamed vegetables or a fresh green salad.

7. Enjoy a heart-healthy meal that is rich in omega-3 fatty acids and low in cholesterol.

Spicy Shrimp and Quinoa Bowl

Time: 30 minutes	Serving Size: 2
Prep Time: 15 minutes	Cook Time: 15 minutes

Nutrition Information Per Serving (1 bowl):

Calories: 320, Carbohydrates: 30g, Saturated Fat: 1.5g, Protein: 25g, Fat: 12g, Sodium: 400mg, Potassium: 500mg, Fiber: 5g, Sugar: 2g, Vitamin C: 30mg, Calcium: 60mg, Iron: 3mg.

Ingredients:

- 1 cup quinoa, rinsed and drained
- 1 pound large shrimp, peeled and deveined
- 2 tablespoons olive oil
- 3 cloves garlic, minced
- 1 teaspoon smoked paprika
- 1/2 teaspoon cayenne pepper (adjust for spice preference)
- 1 teaspoon ground cumin
- Salt and pepper to taste
- 1 cup cherry tomatoes, halved
- 1/2 cup cucumber, diced
- 1/4 cup red onion, finely chopped
- 1/4 cup fresh cilantro, chopped
- 1 avocado, sliced

For the Dressing:

- 2 tablespoons olive oil
- 1 tablespoon fresh lime juice
- 1 teaspoon honey
- Salt and pepper to taste

Directions:

1. In a medium saucepan, combine quinoa with 2 cups of water. Bring to a boil, then reduce heat to low, cover, and simmer for 15 minutes or until the quinoa is cooked and water is absorbed. Fluff with a fork and set aside.

2. In a large bowl, toss the shrimp with minced garlic, smoked paprika, cayenne pepper, ground cumin, salt, and pepper until well coated.

3. Heat olive oil in a skillet over medium-high heat. Add the seasoned shrimp and cook for 2-3 minutes per side or until they are pink and opaque.

4. In a separate bowl, combine the halved cherry tomatoes, diced cucumber, chopped red onion, and fresh cilantro.

5. Whisk together the dressing ingredients in a small bowl: olive oil, fresh lime juice, honey, salt, and pepper.

6. Assemble the bowls by dividing the cooked quinoa between two plates. Top with the spicy shrimp, tomato-cucumber mixture, and sliced avocado.

7. Drizzle the dressing over each bowl.

8. Serve the Spicy Shrimp and Quinoa Bowl immediately, enjoying a flavorful and heart-healthy dish.

Chapter 8: Salads and Side Dishes

Kale and Quinoa Salad with Lemon Vinaigrette

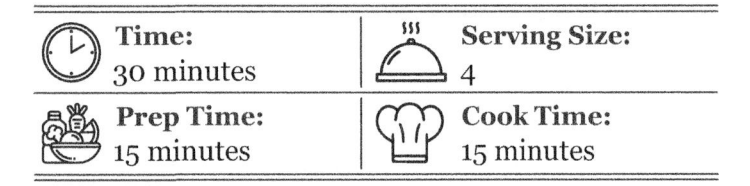

Time: 30 minutes	**Serving Size:** 4
Prep Time: 15 minutes	**Cook Time:** 15 minutes

Nutrition Information Per Serving (1 plate):

Calories: 200, Carbohydrates: 30g, Saturated Fat: 0.5g, Protein: 6g, Fat: 7g, Sodium: 30mg, Potassium: 448mg, Fiber: 5g, Sugar: 3g, Vitamin C: 80mg, Calcium: 55mg, Iron: 2.3mg.

Ingredients:

- 1 cup quinoa, uncooked
- 2 cups water
- 4 cups chopped kale, stems removed
- 1 medium cucumber, diced
- 1/2 red onion, finely chopped
- 1/2 cup chopped almonds
- 1/4 cup olive oil
- Juice of 2 lemons
- 1 tablespoon Dijon mustard
- 1 garlic clove, minced
- Salt and pepper to taste
- Lemon zest for garnish (optional)

Directions:

1. Rinse the quinoa under cold water until the water runs clear. In a medium saucepan, bring 2 cups of water to a boil. Add the quinoa, reduce heat to low, cover, and cook for 15 minutes or until all the water is absorbed. Remove from heat and let it stand for 5 minutes, then fluff with a fork.
2. While the quinoa is cooking, place the kale in a large serving bowl. Massage the kale with your hands for about 2-3 minutes to soften its texture.
3. In a small bowl, whisk together the olive oil, lemon juice, Dijon mustard, minced garlic, and salt and pepper to create the lemon vinaigrette.
4. Add the cooked quinoa, cucumber, red onion, and chopped almonds to the bowl with the kale.
5. Drizzle the lemon vinaigrette over the salad and toss everything to combine. Taste and adjust seasoning as needed.
6. Garnish with lemon zest if desired. Serve immediately or let it sit for flavors to meld.

Roasted Beet and Goat Cheese Salad

Time: 1 hour 10 minutes	**Serving Size:** 4 servings
Prep Time: 10 minutes	**Cook Time:** 1 hour

Nutrition Information Per Serving (1 bowl):

Calories: 210, Carbohydrates: 18g, Saturated Fat: 3.5g, Protein: 7g, Fat: 13g, Sodium: 220mg, Potassium: 400mg, Fiber: 4g, Sugar: 13g, Vitamin C: 6mg, Calcium: 60mg, Iron: 1.2mg.

Ingredients:

- 4 medium beets, cleaned and stems removed
- 1 tablespoon extra-virgin olive oil
- 2 tablespoons balsamic vinegar
- 1 teaspoon Dijon mustard
- 1/2 teaspoon honey (optional, for those not strictly minimizing sugars)
- 1/4 teaspoon black pepper
- 1/8 teaspoon salt
- 4 cups mixed salad greens
- 1/4 cup walnuts, chopped and toasted
- 1/4 cup crumbled goat cheese

Directions:

1. Preheat the oven to 400°F. Wrap beets in aluminum foil and place them on a baking sheet. Roast in the oven for about 1 hour or until beets can be easily pierced with a fork.
2. Remove beets from the oven, unwrap, and let cool. Once cool enough to handle, peel the beets and cut them into wedges.
3. In a small bowl, whisk together the extra-virgin olive oil, balsamic vinegar, Dijon mustard, honey if using, black pepper, and salt to create the dressing.
4. In a large bowl, toss the mixed salad greens with half of the dressing.
5. Arrange the dressed greens on plates. Top each with equal amounts of roasted beet wedges, toasted walnuts, and crumbled goat cheese.
6. Drizzle the remaining dressing over the salads and serve immediately for the freshest taste.

Grilled Vegetable Platter

Time: 30 minutes
Serving Size: 4 servings
Prep Time: 15 minutes
Cook Time: 15 minutes

Nutrition Information Per Serving (1/4 platter):

Calories: 120, Carbohydrates: 15g, Saturated Fat: 1g, Protein: 3g, Fat: 7g, Sodium: 30mg, Potassium: 520mg, Fiber: 4g, Sugar: 6g, Vitamin C: 60mg, Calcium: 30mg, Iron: 1.2mg.

Ingredients:

- 1 medium zucchini, sliced into 1/2 inch rounds
- 1 medium yellow squash, sliced into 1/2 inch rounds
- 1 red bell pepper, seeded and cut into 1-inch pieces
- 1 yellow bell pepper, seeded and cut into 1-inch pieces
- 1 red onion, cut into wedges
- 8 oz. button mushrooms, halved
- 2 tablespoons olive oil
- 1 teaspoon dried oregano
- 1 teaspoon dried basil
- 1/4 teaspoon garlic powder
- Salt and pepper to taste (optional)
- 1 tablespoon balsamic vinegar (optional)

Directions:

1. Preheat your grill to medium-high heat (around 375°F).
2. In a large bowl, combine the zucchini, yellow squash, bell peppers, red onion, and mushrooms.
3. Drizzle the vegetables with olive oil, then season with oregano, basil, garlic powder, and salt and pepper if desired.
4. Toss to coat evenly.
5. Place the vegetables on the grill in a single layer, or use a grill basket if you have one.
6. Grill the vegetables for about 7-8 minutes on

one side until they begin to show grill marks.

7. Flip the vegetables and continue to grill for another 7-8 minutes, until they are tender and nicely charred.

8. Transfer the grilled vegetables to a platter. If desired, drizzle balsamic vinegar over the vegetables for added flavor.

9. Serve the Grilled Vegetable Platter warm or at room temperature as a heart-healthy side dish.

Couscous with Roasted Veggies

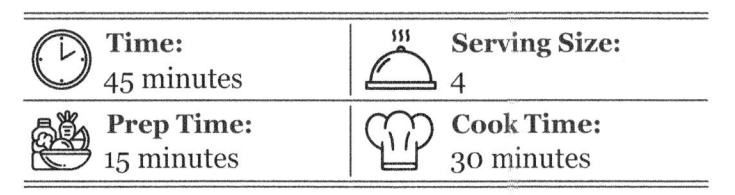

Time: 45 minutes	Serving Size: 4
Prep Time: 15 minutes	Cook Time: 30 minutes

Nutrition Information Per Serving (1 bowl):

Calories: 200, Carbohydrates: 35g, Saturated Fat: 1g, Protein: 6g, Fat: 4g, Sodium: 20mg, Potassium: 450mg, Fiber: 5g, Sugar: 5g, Vitamin C: 30%, Calcium: 4%, Iron: 8%.

Ingredients:

- 1 cup whole wheat couscous
- 2 cups low-sodium vegetable broth
- 1 medium zucchini, cubed
- 1 red bell pepper, chopped
- 1 yellow bell pepper, chopped
- 1 small red onion, sliced
- 2 tablespoons extra virgin olive oil
- 1 teaspoon smoked paprika
- ½ teaspoon ground cumin
- ½ teaspoon garlic powder
- Salt and pepper, to taste
- 1/4 cup chopped fresh parsley
- Juice of 1 lemon

Directions:

1. Preheat your oven to 425°F.

2. On a baking sheet, toss the zucchini, red and yellow bell peppers, and red onion with extra virgin olive oil, smoked paprika, ground cumin, garlic powder, salt, and pepper until all the veggies are well coated.

3. Roast in the oven for about 25-30 minutes, or until vegetables are tender and have a nice char.

4. Meanwhile, bring the low-sodium vegetable broth to a boil in a medium saucepan. Stir in the couscous, cover, and remove from heat. Let it stand for about 5 minutes, then fluff with a fork.

5. Once the vegetables are roasted, remove from the oven and let them cool slightly.

6. In a large bowl, combine the fluffed couscous with the roasted veggies. Add fresh parsley and drizzle with lemon juice. Toss everything together until well mixed.

7. Taste and adjust seasoning if necessary, then serve either warm or at room temperature as a delicious and heart-healthy side dish.

Sweet Corn and Black Bean Salad

Time: 25 minutes	Serving Size: 4 servings
Prep Time: 15 minutes	Cook Time: 10 minutes

Nutrition Information Per Serving (1 bowl):

Calories: 200, Carbohydrates: 37g, Saturated Fat: 0.5g, Protein: 8g, Fat: 3g, Sodium: 10mg, Potassium: 500mg, Fiber: 9g, Sugar: 5g, Vitamin C: 20mg, Calcium: 30mg, Iron: 2mg.

Ingredients:

- 1 cup sweet corn, fresh or frozen
- 1 (15-ounce) can black beans, drained and rinsed
- 1 red bell pepper,

- diced
- 1 avocado, diced
- 1/4 cup fresh cilantro, chopped
- 1 lime, juiced
- 1 tablespoon extra virgin olive oil
- 1/2 teaspoon ground cumin
- Salt and pepper to taste

Directions:

1. Begin by cooking the sweet corn. If using fresh corn, remove the kernels from the cob. If using frozen, thaw it first. In a saucepan, bring water to a boil and cook the corn for about 5 minutes or until tender. Drain and allow it to cool.
2. In a large mixing bowl, combine the cooled corn, black beans, and diced red bell pepper. Toss these ingredients together until they are well mixed.
3. Next, take the ripe avocado and cut it in half, removing the pit and skin. Dice the avocado into small cubes and add it to the bowl. Gently fold the avocado into the salad to prevent it from becoming mushy.
4. Now, add the fresh cilantro to the mixture for a burst of flavor. Finely chop the cilantro before incorporating it into the salad.
5. For the dressing, whisk together the juice of one lime, extra virgin olive oil, and ground cumin in a small bowl. Season with salt and pepper according to your taste preference.
6. Pour the dressing over the salad and toss everything together until the ingredients are evenly coated with the dressing.
7. Serve the Sweet Corn and Black Bean Salad chilled or at room temperature as a refreshing side dish or a light main course.
8. Enjoy your heart-healthy, flavorful salad that's perfect for anyone looking to maintain low cholesterol levels while still enjoying delicious food.

Asparagus with Balsamic Tomatoes

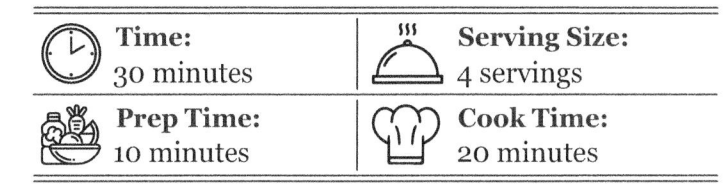

Time: 30 minutes	Serving Size: 4 servings
Prep Time: 10 minutes	Cook Time: 20 minutes

Nutrition Information Per Serving (1 serving unit):

Calories: 150, Carbohydrates: 18g, Saturated Fat: 1g, Protein: 5g, Fat: 7g, Sodium: 30mg, Potassium: 400mg, Fiber: 4g, Sugar: 6g, Vitamin C: 20mg, Calcium: 40mg, Iron: 2mg.

Ingredients:

- 1 pound asparagus, trimmed
- 2 tablespoons extra virgin olive oil
- 1 pint cherry tomatoes, halved
- 2 tablespoons balsamic vinegar
- 1 teaspoon mustard
- 1 garlic clove, minced
- Salt and freshly ground black pepper, to taste
- 1 tablespoon fresh basil, chopped
- 1 tablespoon pine nuts (optional)

Directions:

1. Preheat your oven to 400°F.
2. Arrange the asparagus on a baking sheet and drizzle with 1 tablespoon of the olive oil. Season with salt and pepper, and toss to coat.
3. Roast in the preheated oven for about 15 minutes, or until the asparagus is tender and slightly crispy.
4. Meanwhile, in a small bowl, whisk together the balsamic vinegar, mustard, and minced garlic to create a dressing.
5. Heat the remaining 1 tablespoon of olive oil

in a skillet over medium heat. Add the cherry tomatoes and cook for about 5 minutes, until they are warm and begin to soften.

6. Remove the asparagus from the oven and place it on a serving platter.
7. Spoon the warm tomatoes over the asparagus.
8. Drizzle the balsamic dressing over the asparagus and tomatoes.
9. Garnish with chopped basil and pine nuts if using.
10. Serve immediately.

Greek Salad with Low-Fat Feta

Time: 20 minutes	Serving Size: 4 servings
Prep Time: 15 minutes	Cook Time: 5 minutes

Nutrition Information Per Serving (1 bowl):

Calories: 150, Carbohydrates: 10g, Saturated Fat: 2g, Protein: 6g, Fat: 10g, Sodium: 200mg, Potassium: 300mg, Fiber: 3g, Sugar: 4g, Vitamin C: 20mg, Calcium: 150mg, Iron: 1mg.

Ingredients:

- 1 large cucumber, peeled and diced
- 3 medium tomatoes, diced
- 1 medium red onion, thinly sliced
- 1/2 cup Kalamata olives, pitted and halved
- 1 cup low-fat feta cheese, crumbled
- 1/4 cup fresh parsley, chopped
- 2 tablespoons extra virgin olive oil
- 1 tablespoon red wine vinegar
- 1 teaspoon dried oregano
- Salt and pepper to taste

Directions:

1. In a large mixing bowl, combine the peeled and diced cucumber, diced tomatoes, and thinly sliced red onion.
2. Add the pitted and halved Kalamata olives and crumbled low-fat feta cheese to the mixture.
3. In a small bowl, whisk together the extra virgin olive oil, red wine vinegar, dried oregano, salt, and pepper to create the dressing.
4. Pour the dressing over the vegetable and feta mixture and gently toss to coat all the ingredients evenly.
5. Sprinkle the chopped fresh parsley over the salad and give it one final toss.
6. Let the salad sit for about 5 minutes to allow the flavors to meld together.
7. Serve the Greek Salad with Low-Fat Feta as a refreshing side dish or a light main course.

Cauliflower Rice Pilaf

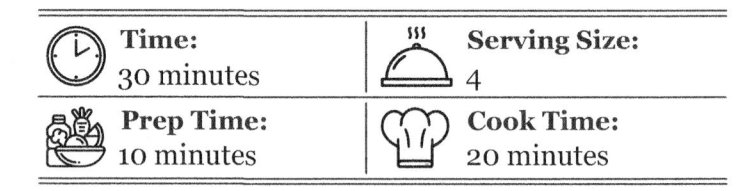

Time: 30 minutes	Serving Size: 4
Prep Time: 10 minutes	Cook Time: 20 minutes

Nutrition Information Per Serving (1 cup):

Calories: 120, Carbohydrates: 15g, Saturated Fat: 0.5g, Protein: 4g, Fat: 5g, Sodium: 150mg, Potassium: 430mg, Fiber: 3g, Sugar: 5g, Vitamin C: 60mg, Calcium: 40mg, Iron: 1.2mg.

Ingredients:

- 1 medium head of cauliflower
- 2 tablespoons of extra virgin olive oil
- 1 small onion, finely chopped
- 2 cloves of garlic, minced
- 1/4 cup of chopped parsley
- 1/2 teaspoon of ground cumin
- 1/2 teaspoon of salt
- 1/4 teaspoon of pepper

- 1/2 cup of vegetable broth
- 1/4 cup of slivered almonds, toasted
- 2 tablespoons of raisins (optional)
- Lemon wedges for serving (optional)

Directions:

1. Start by washing the cauliflower head and drying it thoroughly. Grate the cauliflower florets on the large holes of a box grater or pulse them in a food processor until they reach the consistency of rice.
2. Heat the extra virgin olive oil in a large skillet over medium heat. Add the finely chopped onion and minced garlic, sautéing until the onion is translucent, about 3-4 minutes.
3. Stir in the cauliflower rice, and cook for another 5-7 minutes, until it begins to soften. Sprinkle in the ground cumin, salt, and pepper, mixing well to combine.
4. Pour in the vegetable broth, reduce the heat to low, cover, and let simmer for about 10 minutes, or until the cauliflower is tender and the liquid is absorbed.
5. Remove from heat, and fluff the cauliflower rice with a fork. Gently fold in the chopped parsley, toasted slivered almonds, and raisins if using.
6. Serve warm with lemon wedges on the side for a refreshing zest, if desired.

Broccoli and Apple Salad with Walnuts

Time: 20 minutes
Serving Size: 4 servings
Prep Time: 15 minutes
Cook Time: 5 minutes

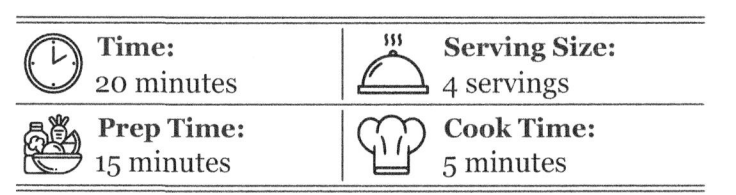

Nutrition Information Per Serving (1 bowl):
Calories: 165, Carbohydrates: 19g, Saturated Fat: 1g, Protein: 4g, Fat: 9g, Sodium: 55mg, Potassium: 300mg, Fiber: 4g, Sugar: 10g, Vitamin C: 80%, Calcium: 5%, Iron: 6%.

Ingredients:

- 4 cups of broccoli florets
- 1 large apple, cored and sliced into thin matchsticks
- 1/2 cup of walnuts, roughly chopped
- 1/4 cup of red onion, finely diced
- 2 tablespoons of apple cider vinegar
- 1 tablespoon of honey (or maple syrup for a vegan option)
- 1 teaspoon of Dijon mustard
- 2 tablespoons of extra virgin olive oil
- Salt and pepper to taste

Directions:

1. Start by steaming the broccoli florets. Bring a pot of water fitted with a steamer basket to a boil, then add the broccoli and steam for about 3-4 minutes until they are bright green and slightly tender. Once done, remove from heat and allow them to cool.
2. In a large mixing bowl, combine the cooled broccoli, apple matchsticks, and red onion.
3. In a separate small bowl, whisk together the apple cider vinegar, honey, and Dijon mustard until well blended. Slowly drizzle in the extra virgin olive oil, whisking continuously to create an emulsified dressing. Season the dressing with salt and pepper to your liking.
4. Pour the dressing over the broccoli and apple mixture, and toss until everything is well coated.
5. Finally, add the walnuts to the salad and give it another gentle toss to distribute them evenly.

CHAPTER 8: SALADS AND SIDE DISHES

6. Serve the salad immediately, or let it chill in the refrigerator for about an hour to allow the flavors to meld together.

Roasted Carrot and Avocado Salad

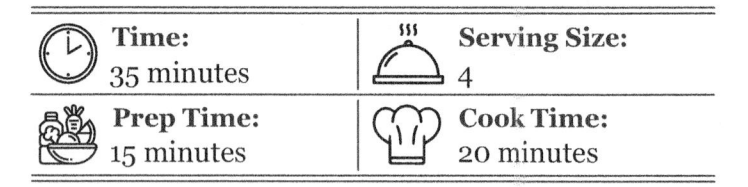

🕐 Time: 35 minutes	🍽 Serving Size: 4
🥗 Prep Time: 15 minutes	👨‍🍳 Cook Time: 20 minutes

Nutrition Information Per Serving (1 plate):

Calories: 220, Carbohydrates: 18g, Saturated Fat: 2g, Protein: 3g, Fat: 16g, Sodium: 110mg, Potassium: 487mg, Fiber: 7g, Sugar: 5g, Vitamin C: 14mg, Calcium: 51mg, Iron: 1mg.

Ingredients:

- 8 medium carrots, peeled and sliced lengthwise
- 2 tablespoons extra virgin olive oil
- ½ teaspoon ground cumin
- Salt and pepper to taste
- 2 ripe avocados, pitted and sliced
- 1 small red onion, thinly sliced
- 2 tablespoons lemon juice
- ¼ cup chopped fresh cilantro
- 1 tablespoon pumpkin seeds
- 1 tablespoon sesame seeds

Directions:

1. Preheat your oven to 400°F (200°C).
2. In a mixing bowl, toss the carrots with 1 tablespoon of extra virgin olive oil, ground cumin, salt, and pepper until well coated.
3. Spread the seasoned carrots in a single layer on a baking sheet and roast for 20 minutes, or until tender and slightly caramelized.
4. While the carrots are roasting, arrange the sliced avocados and red onion on a serving platter.
5. Remove the carrots from the oven and let them cool slightly.
6. Place the roasted carrots on top of the avocados and onions.
7. Drizzle the remaining tablespoon of olive oil and the lemon juice over the salad.
8. Garnish with chopped cilantro, pumpkin seeds, and sesame seeds.
9. Serve warm or at room temperature for a heart-healthy and flavorful side dish.

Spinach and Strawberry Salad

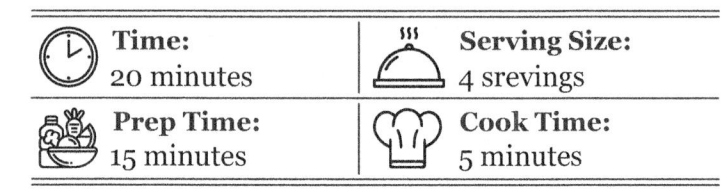

🕐 Time: 20 minutes	🍽 Serving Size: 4 srevings
🥗 Prep Time: 15 minutes	👨‍🍳 Cook Time: 5 minutes

Nutrition Information Per Serving (1 bowl):

Calories: 150, Carbohydrates: 18g, Saturated Fat: 0.5g, Protein: 4g, Fat: 8g, Sodium: 130mg, Potassium: 470mg, Fiber: 4g, Sugar: 7g, Vitamin C: 90mg, Calcium: 75mg, Iron: 2mg.

Ingredients:

- 4 cups fresh baby spinach
- 1 cup sliced strawberries
- 1/4 cup sliced almonds, toasted
- 1/4 cup crumbled feta cheese, low-fat
- 1/4 red onion, thinly sliced
- 2 tablespoons extra virgin olive oil
- 1 tablespoon balsamic vinegar
- 1 teaspoon honey
- 1/2 teaspoon Dijon mustard
- Salt and pepper to taste

Directions:

1. Begin by washing the baby spinach thoroughly and patting it dry with a clean kitchen towel. Place the spinach in a large salad bowl.

2. Wash the strawberries and slice them. Add the sliced strawberries to the bowl with the spinach.

3. In a small pan over medium heat, toast the sliced almonds for about 3 to 5 minutes, or until they are golden brown and fragrant. Be sure to stir frequently to prevent burning.

4. Once toasted, add the almonds to the salad bowl.

5. Add the crumbled low-fat feta cheese and thinly sliced red onion to the salad bowl.

6. In a small mixing bowl, whisk together the extra virgin olive oil, balsamic vinegar, honey, and Dijon mustard to create the dressing. Season with salt and pepper according to your preference.

7. Drizzle the dressing over the salad and toss gently to combine all the ingredients.

8. Serve the salad immediately, or chill it in the refrigerator for a short time if you prefer it cold.

Butternut Squash Soup

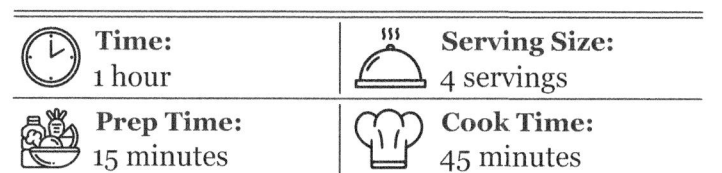

Time: 1 hour
Serving Size: 4 servings
Prep Time: 15 minutes
Cook Time: 45 minutes

Nutrition Information Per Serving (1 bowl):

Calories: 165, Carbohydrates: 27g, Saturated Fat: 0.5g, Protein: 3g, Fat: 6g, Sodium: 180mg, Potassium: 670mg, Fiber: 5g, Sugar: 5g, Vitamin C: 35mg, Calcium: 100mg, Iron: 1.4mg.

Ingredients:

- 1 medium butternut squash (about 2 pounds), peeled, seeded, and chopped into 1-inch cubes
- 2 tablespoons extra virgin olive oil
- 1 medium onion, diced
- 2 cloves of garlic, minced
- 4 cups low-sodium vegetable broth
- 1 teaspoon dried thyme
- 1/2 teaspoon ground cinnamon
- 1/4 teaspoon nutmeg
- Salt and pepper to taste
- Fresh parsley for garnish (optional)

Directions:

1. Preheat your oven to 400°F.

2. Place the butternut squash on a baking sheet and drizzle with 1 tablespoon of extra virgin olive oil. Toss to coat and roast in the preheated oven for 25 minutes or until tender and lightly browned.

3. While the squash is roasting, heat the remaining tablespoon of olive oil in a large pot over medium heat. Add the diced onion and minced garlic, cooking until the onion becomes translucent, about 5 minutes.

4. To the pot, add the roasted butternut squash, low-sodium vegetable broth, dried thyme, ground cinnamon, and nutmeg. Stir well to combine.

5. Bring the mixture to a boil, then reduce the heat and simmer for 20 minutes, allowing the flavors to meld together.

6. After simmering, use an immersion blender to puree the soup until smooth. Alternatively, you can carefully transfer the soup to a blender and puree it in batches.

7. Season the soup with salt and pepper to taste. Serve hot, garnished with fresh parsley if desired.

Green Beans Almondine

⏰ **Time:** 25 minutes	🍽 **Serving Size:** 4
🥗 **Prep Time:** 10 minutes	👨‍🍳 **Cook Time:** 15 minutes

Nutrition Information Per Serving (1 serving):

Calories: 150, Carbohydrates: 8g, Saturated Fat: 1g, Protein: 4g, Fat: 12g, Sodium: 30mg, Potassium: 239mg, Fiber: 3g, Sugar: 2g, Vitamin C: 12.7mg, Calcium: 55mg, Iron: 1.1mg.

Ingredients:

- 1 pound fresh green beans, trimmed
- 2 tablespoons slivered almonds
- 2 tablespoons extra virgin olive oil
- 1 tablespoon lemon juice
- 2 cloves garlic, minced
- Salt and pepper to taste
- 1 teaspoon grated lemon zest (optional for garnish)

Directions:

1. Preheat your oven to 350°F.
2. Spread slivered almonds on a baking sheet and toast in the oven for 5-7 minutes until they are golden brown. Be sure to watch them closely to avoid burning. Once toasted, set aside to cool.
3. While the almonds are toasting, boil a pot of water and blanch the green beans for 2-3 minutes until they are bright green and tender-crisp.
4. Drain and immediately plunge them into an ice bath to stop the cooking process and retain their vibrant color.
5. In a large skillet over medium heat, warm the extra virgin olive oil, then add the minced garlic and sauté for about 1 minute until fragrant, being careful not to burn the garlic.
6. Add the blanched green beans to the skillet and sauté for another 2-3 minutes. Season with salt and pepper to taste.
7. Remove from heat, drizzle with lemon juice, and toss to coat evenly.
8. Serve the green beans topped with toasted slivered almonds and optional lemon zest for garnish.

Chapter 9: Desserts

Baked Apples with Cinnamon

⏱ Time: 45 minutes	🍽 Serving Size: 4 apples
🥗 Prep Time: 15 minutes	👨‍🍳 Cook Time: 30 minutes

Nutrition Information Per Serving (1 apple):

Calories: 190, Carbohydrates: 50g, Saturated Fat: 0g, Protein: 0.5g, Fat: 0.2g, Sodium: 2mg, Potassium: 194mg, Fiber: 5g, Sugar: 44g, Vitamin C: 8.4mg, Calcium: 11mg, Iron: 0.3mg.

Ingredients:

- 4 large apples, firm variety such as Fuji or Honeycrisp
- 1/4 cup brown sugar, packed
- 1 tsp ground cinnamon
- 1/4 tsp ground nutmeg
- 1/4 tsp ground ginger
- 1/2 cup water
- Optional toppings: chopped nuts or a dollop of low-fat Greek yogurt

Directions:

1. Preheat your oven to 350°F (175°C).
2. Begin by coring the apples, removing the seeds and creating a hollow space in the middle for the filling. Be careful not to pierce through the bottom of the apples.
3. In a small bowl, combine the brown sugar, ground cinnamon, ground nutmeg, and ground ginger.
4. Stuff each apple with an equal amount of the sugar and spice mixture.
5. Place the stuffed apples upright in a baking dish and pour the water into the bottom of the dish around the apples.
6. Bake in the preheated oven for 30 minutes or until the apples are soft and the filling has caramelized.
7. Carefully remove the baking dish from the oven and allow the apples to cool for a few minutes.
8. Serve the baked apples warm, with optional toppings of chopped nuts or a dollop of low-fat Greek yogurt, if desired.

Low-Fat Berry Yogurt Parfait

⏱ Time: 10 minutes	🍽 Serving Size: 1
🥗 Prep Time: 10 minutes	👨‍🍳 Cook Time: 0 minutes

Nutrition Information Per Serving (1 glass):

Calories: 150, Carbohydrates: 22g, Saturated Fat: 0.5g, Protein: 8g, Fat: 2g, Sodium: 60mg, Potassium: 200mg, Fiber: 3g, Sugar: 18g, Vitamin C: 40%, Calcium: 15%, Iron: 5%.

Ingredients:

- 1 cup fat-free or 1% low-fat Greek yogurt
- ½ cup fresh blueberries
- ½ cup fresh strawberries, sliced
- ¼ cup whole grain granola
- 1 tablespoon honey (optional)
- A sprig of fresh mint for garnish (optional)

Directions:

1. Begin by gathering all your ingredients.
2. Take a serving glass and start layering your parfait with a spoonful of Greek yogurt at the bottom.
3. Next, add a layer of fresh blueberries. Add another layer of yogurt, then a layer of sliced strawberries.
4. Sprinkle a layer of whole grain granola over the strawberries for a bit of crunch.
5. Repeat the layering process until the glass is almost full, finishing with a layer of granola on top.
6. Drizzle a tablespoon of honey over the granola if desired for extra sweetness.
7. Garnish with a sprig of fresh mint to add a touch of elegance and additional flavor. Serve immediately to enjoy the parfait's freshness and textural contrast.

Dark Chocolate-Dipped Strawberries

Time: 15 minutes	Serving Size: 4 servings
Prep Time: 10 minutes	Cook Time: 5 minutes

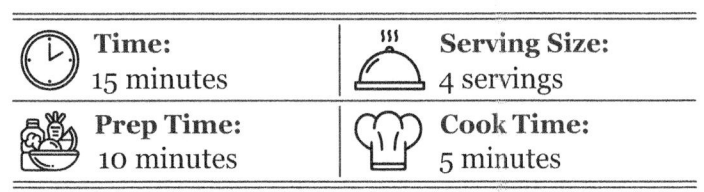

Nutrition Information Per Serving (1 serving unit):

Calories: 150, Carbohydrates: 20g, Saturated Fat: 3g, Protein: 2g, Fat: 8g, Sodium: 20mg, Potassium: 150mg, Fiber: 3g, Sugar: 15g, Vitamin C: 50mg, Calcium: 20mg, Iron: 1mg.

Ingredients:

- 1 cup of dark chocolate chips (preferably 70% cocoa or higher)
- 1 pint fresh strawberries, washed and dried
- 1 teaspoon coconut oil
- Optional toppings: chopped nuts, coconut flakes, or sea salt

Directions:

1. Line a baking sheet with parchment paper and set aside.
2. In a microwave-safe bowl, combine the dark chocolate chips and coconut oil. Microwave in 30-second intervals, stirring in between, until completely melted and smooth. Be careful not to overheat.
3. Holding a strawberry by the stem, dip it into the melted chocolate, letting the excess drip off.
4. Place the chocolate-dipped strawberry onto the prepared baking sheet. If desired, sprinkle with optional toppings such as chopped nuts, coconut flakes, or a pinch of sea salt.
5. Repeat with the remaining strawberries.
6. Place the baking sheet in the refrigerator for about 5 minutes or until the chocolate has set.
7. Enjoy your heart-healthy dessert!

Banana Bread with Almond Flour

Time: 1 hour 5 minutes	Serving Size: 10 servings
Prep Time: 15 minutes	Cook Time: 50 minutes

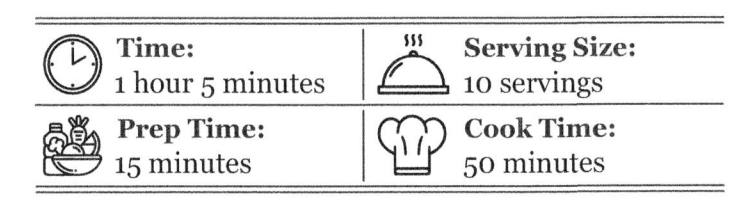

Nutrition Information Per Serving (1 piece of bread):

Calories: 190, Carbohydrates: 18g, Saturated Fat: 1g, Protein: 6g, Fat: 12g, Sodium: 140mg, Potassium: 200mg, Fiber: 3g, Sugar: 8g, Vitamin C: 1.2mg, Calcium: 60mg, Iron: 1.2mg.

Ingredients:

- 3 ripe bananas, mashed
- 2 cups almond flour
- 3 large eggs
- 1/4 cup unsweetened applesauce
- 1 tsp baking soda
- 1/2 tsp salt
- 1/4 cup honey
- 1 tsp vanilla extract
- 1/2 tsp cinnamon (optional)

Directions:

1. Preheat your oven to 350°F (175°C).
2. In a large bowl, combine the mashed bananas with the eggs, unsweetened applesauce, honey, and vanilla extract, mixing until well blended.
3. In a separate bowl, whisk together the almond flour, baking soda, salt, and cinnamon if you're using it.
4. Gradually fold the dry ingredients into the wet mixture, stirring until just combined.
5. Be careful not to overmix. Pour the batter into a greased 9x5-inch loaf pan.
6. Bake in the preheated oven for 50 minutes or until a toothpick inserted into the center comes out clean.
7. Let the banana bread cool in the pan for about 10 minutes before transferring it to a wire rack to cool completely.
8. Slice, serve, and enjoy your low cholesterol, heart-healthy dessert!

Peach and Blueberry Crumble

Time: 45 minutes		Serving Size: 6	
Prep Time: 15 minutes		Cook Time: 30 minutes	

Nutrition Information Per Serving (1/6 of dish):

Calories: 210, Carbohydrates: 38g, Saturated Fat: 1g, Protein: 3g, Fat: 6g, Sodium: 10mg, Potassium: 200mg, Fiber: 5g, Sugar: 22g, Vitamin C: 10mg, Calcium: 20mg, Iron: 1.2mg.

Ingredients:

- 3 cups fresh peaches, peeled and sliced
- 1 cup fresh blueberries
- Juice of half a lemon
- 2 tablespoons honey
- 1 teaspoon vanilla extract
- 1 cup rolled oats
- 1/2 cup almond flour
- 1/4 cup chopped walnuts
- 1/4 cup coconut oil, melted
- 2 tablespoons ground flaxseed
- 1 teaspoon cinnamon
- Pinch of salt

Directions:

1. Preheat your oven to 350°F (175°C).
2. In a large bowl, combine the peeled and sliced peaches, fresh blueberries, juice of half a lemon, and honey. Mix well until the fruit is evenly coated.
3. Stir the vanilla extract into the fruit mixture, then spread it out evenly in a baking dish.
4. In a separate bowl, mix together the rolled oats, almond flour, chopped walnuts, and melted coconut oil until the mixture becomes crumbly.
5. To the oat mixture, add ground flaxseed, cinnamon, and a pinch of salt. Combine these ingredients thoroughly.
6. Sprinkle the oat mixture over the fruit in the

baking dish, covering it completely.

7. Place the baking dish in the preheated oven and bake for about 30 minutes or until the topping is golden brown and the fruit is bubbling.

8. Once done, remove the crumble from the oven and let it cool slightly before serving.

Carrot Cake with Low-Fat Cream Cheese Frosting

Time: 1 hour 30 minutes	Serving Size: 12 servings
Prep Time: 30 minutes	Cook Time: 60 minutes

Nutrition Information Per Serving (1 slice):

Calories: 250, Carbohydrates: 35g, Saturated Fat: 2g, Protein: 6g, Fat: 10g, Sodium: 220mg, Potassium: 120mg, Fiber: 3g, Sugar: 20g, Vitamin C: 1mg, Calcium: 60mg, Iron: 1.2mg.

Ingredients:

- 2 cups whole wheat flour
- 1 teaspoon baking soda
- 1/2 teaspoon salt
- 1 1/2 teaspoons ground cinnamon
- 1/2 cup unsweetened applesauce
- 1/4 cup canola oil
- 1 cup granulated sugar
- 1/2 cup brown sugar
- 3 large eggs
- 2 teaspoons vanilla extract
- 2 cups grated carrots
- 1/2 cup crushed pineapple, drained

For the Frosting:

- 8 ounces low-fat cream cheese, softened
- 1/4 cup unsalted butter, softened
- 2 cups powdered sugar
- 1 teaspoon vanilla extract

Directions:

1. Preheat your oven to 350°F (175°C). Grease and flour a 9x13 inch baking pan.

2. In a large bowl, whisk together the whole wheat flour, baking soda, salt, and ground cinnamon. Set this dry mixture aside.

3. In a separate bowl, beat together the unsweetened applesauce, canola oil, granulated sugar, and brown sugar until well blended. Add the eggs one at a time, beating well after each addition, then stir in the vanilla extract.

4. Gradually add the dry ingredients to the wet ingredients, mixing until just combined. Fold in the grated carrots and crushed pineapple until everything is well incorporated.

5. Pour the batter into the prepared baking pan. Bake for about 60 minutes, or until a toothpick inserted into the center comes out clean. Allow the cake to cool completely before frosting.

6. For the frosting, beat the low-fat cream cheese and unsalted butter together in a bowl until smooth and creamy. Gradually add the powdered sugar and vanilla extract, continue beating until the frosting is fluffy.

7. Once the cake is cool, spread the frosting evenly over the top. Slice into 12 equal pieces and serve.

Almond and Date Energy Balls

Time: 20 minutes	Serving Size: 12 balls
Prep Time: 15 minutes	Cook Time: 5 minutes

Nutrition Information Per Serving (1 ball):

Calories: 120, Carbohydrates: 18g, Saturated Fat: 0.5g, Protein: 3g, Fat: 5g, Sodium: 0mg,

Potassium: 200mg, Fiber: 3g, Sugar: 14g, Vitamin C: 0.1mg, Calcium: 40mg, Iron: 1mg.

Ingredients:

- 1 cup raw almonds
- 1 cup pitted dates
- 1/4 cup unsweetened shredded coconut
- 1 tbsp chia seeds
- 1/4 tsp ground cinnamon
- A pinch of salt
- 2 tbsp water, if needed

Directions:

1. Place the raw almonds in a food processor and pulse until they are finely chopped.
2. Add the pitted dates, shredded coconut, chia seeds, ground cinnamon, and a pinch of salt to the food processor.
3. Process until the mixture sticks together when pinched, adding 1 tablespoon of water at a time if the mixture is too dry.
4. Remove the blade from the food processor and scoop out tablespoon-sized amounts of the mixture.
5. Using your hands, roll the mixture into balls.
6. Place the balls on a baking sheet lined with parchment paper and refrigerate for at least 5 minutes to firm up before serving.
7. Store the energy balls in an airtight container in the refrigerator for up to a week.

Vegan Chocolate Mousse

Time: 15 minutes
Serving Size: 2
Prep Time: 10 minutes
Cook Time: 5 minutes

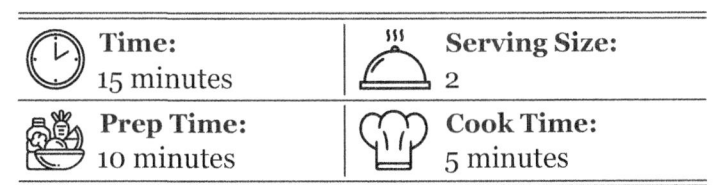

Nutrition Information Per Serving (1 serving unit):

Calories: 200, Carbohydrates: 25g, Saturated Fat: 1g, Protein: 4g, Fat: 11g, Sodium: 15mg, Potassium: 300mg, Fiber: 7g, Sugar: 12g, Vitamin C: 0.2mg, Calcium: 20mg, Iron: 3.6mg.

Ingredients:

- 2 large ripe avocados, peeled and pitted
- 1/4 cup raw cacao powder
- 1/4 cup unsweetened almond milk
- 1/3 cup pure maple syrup
- 1 teaspoon pure vanilla extract
- A pinch of sea salt
- Fresh raspberries, for garnish (optional)

Directions:

1. In a blender or food processor, combine the ripe avocados, raw cacao powder, unsweetened almond milk, pure maple syrup, pure vanilla extract, and a pinch of sea salt.
2. Blend on high until the mixture is smooth and creamy, which should take about 1 minute.
3. Pause to scrape down the sides with a spatula as necessary to ensure all ingredients are well incorporated.
4. Once the mixture is fully combined and smooth, divide it into two serving dishes. For the best texture, chill the mousse in the refrigerator for at least 30 minutes before serving.
5. If desired, garnish with fresh raspberries just before serving to add a pop of color and a burst of tart flavor that complements the rich chocolate. Enjoy your heart-healthy and indulgent treat!
6. Remember to store any leftovers in an airtight container in the refrigerator. The mousse can be kept for up to 2 days, making it a perfect make-ahead dessert for any occasion.

Fruit Salad with Mint and Honey

Time: 15 minutes
Serving Size: 4
Prep Time: 15 minutes
Cook Time: 0 minutes

Nutrition Information Per Serving (1 serving):

Calories: 120, Carbohydrates: 31g, Saturated Fat: 0g, Protein: 1g, Fat: 0g, Sodium: 5mg, Potassium: 200mg, Fiber: 3g, Sugar: 25g, Vitamin C: 60%, Calcium: 2%, Iron: 2%.

Ingredients:

- 2 cups of mixed berries (strawberries, blueberries, raspberries)
- 1 medium banana, sliced
- 1 apple, cored and chopped
- 1 orange, peeled and sectioned
- 1 tablespoon of fresh mint leaves, finely chopped
- 2 tablespoons of honey
- Juice of 1 lemon

Directions:

1. Begin by washing the mixed berries thoroughly and gently patting them dry. Place them into a large mixing bowl.
2. Peel the banana and slice it into rounds, then add to the bowl with the berries.
3. Core the apple and chop it into bite-sized pieces, adding it to the mixing bowl as well.
4. Peel the orange, making sure to remove any pith, and separate it into sections. Add the orange sections to the salad.
5. Take the fresh mint leaves and finely chop them, sprinkling the mint over the fruit in the bowl.
6. Drizzle 2 tablespoons of honey evenly over the fruit.
7. Cut the lemon in half and squeeze its juice over the fruit, making sure to avoid any seeds falling into the bowl.
8. Gently toss all the ingredients together until the fruit is evenly coated with the mint, honey, and lemon juice.
9. Serve immediately or cover and refrigerate for up to 2 hours to let the flavors meld together before serving.

Oatmeal Raisin Cookies (Low Sugar)

Time: 30 minutes
Serving Size: 12 cookies
Prep Time: 15 minutes
Cook Time: 15 minutes

Nutrition Information Per Serving (1 cookie):

Calories: 100, Carbohydrates: 15g, Saturated Fat: 0.5g, Protein: 2g, Fat: 3.5g, Sodium: 75mg, Potassium: 90mg, Fiber: 2g, Sugar: 5g, Vitamin C: 0mg, Calcium: 20mg, Iron: 0.7mg.

Ingredients:

- 1 cup rolled oats
- 3/4 cup whole wheat flour
- 1 1/2 tsp baking powder
- 1 1/2 tsp cinnamon
- 1/4 tsp salt
- 2 tbsp unsalted butter, melted and cooled
- 1 large egg
- 1 tsp vanilla extract
- 1/4 cup honey
- 1/2 cup unsweetened applesauce
- 1/2 cup raisins

Directions:

1. Preheat your oven to 325°F (163°C). Line a baking sheet with parchment paper.
2. In a medium bowl, whisk together oats, whole wheat flour, baking powder, cinnamon, and salt.

3. In another bowl, whisk together the melted butter, egg, and vanilla extract. Stir in the honey and unsweetened applesauce until well combined.

4. Add the wet ingredients to the dry ingredients and stir until just combined. Fold in the raisins.

5. Drop tablespoonfuls of the dough onto the prepared baking sheet, flattening each cookie slightly with the back of the spoon.

6. Bake in the preheated oven for 15 minutes or until the edges are lightly browned.

7. Remove from the oven and let the cookies cool on the baking sheet for 5 minutes, then transfer to a wire rack to cool completely.

Pumpkin Pie with Whole Wheat Crust

Time: 1 hour 30 minutes	Serving Size: 8
Prep Time: 30 minutes	Cook Time: 1 hour

Nutrition Information Per Serving (1 slice):

Calories: 250, Carbohydrates: 35g, Saturated Fat: 2g, Protein: 6g, Fat: 10g, Sodium: 200mg, Potassium: 200mg, Fiber: 5g, Sugar: 16g, Vitamin C: 2mg, Calcium: 50mg, Iron: 1.8mg.

Ingredients:

- 1 cup whole wheat flour
- 1/4 cup cold butter, cut into small pieces
- 1/4 teaspoon salt
- 2-3 tablespoons ice water
- 1 15-ounce can pure pumpkin puree
- 3 large eggs
- 1/4 cup honey
- 1 teaspoon cinnamon
- 1/2 teaspoon ginger
- 1/4 teaspoon nutmeg
- 1/4 teaspoon cloves
- 1/2 teaspoon salt
- 3/4 cup unsweetened almond milk

Directions:

1. Preheat your oven to 375°F. In a mixing bowl, combine the whole wheat flour and 1/4 teaspoon salt.

2. Add the cold butter pieces, using a pastry cutter or fork to blend into the flour until the mixture resembles coarse crumbs.

3. Drizzle in ice water, 1 tablespoon at a time, until the dough comes together when pressed.

4. Roll out the dough on a floured surface into a 12-inch circle. Transfer it to a 9-inch pie plate, trim any excess, and crimp the edges. Refrigerate the crust while you prepare the filling.

5. For the filling, in a large bowl, whisk together the pumpkin puree, eggs, honey, cinnamon, ginger, nutmeg, cloves, and 1/2 teaspoon salt until well combined. Gradually stir in the almond milk.

6. Pour the filling into the prepared pie crust. Bake for 60 minutes, or until the filling is set and a knife inserted near the center comes out clean.

7. Allow the pie to cool completely on a wire rack before slicing and serving.

Grilled Pineapple with Honey Drizzle

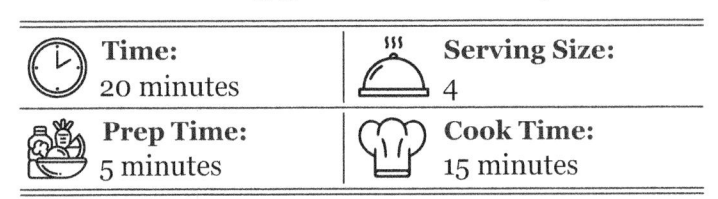

Time: 20 minutes	Serving Size: 4
Prep Time: 5 minutes	Cook Time: 15 minutes

Nutrition Information Per Serving (1 slice):

Calories: 150, Carbohydrates: 22g, Saturated Fat: 0g, Protein: 1g, Fat: 0.5g, Sodium: 2mg,

Potassium: 165mg, Fiber: 2g, Sugar: 17g, Vitamin C: 79%, Calcium: 2%, Iron: 2%.

Ingredients:

- 1 fresh pineapple, peeled, cored, and cut into 4 rings
- 2 tablespoons honey
- 1 teaspoon cinnamon
- Cooking spray or a small amount of olive oil for grilling

Directions:

1. Preheat your grill to medium-high heat (around 375°F).
2. While heating the grill, prepare the pineapple. Peel, core, and cut the pineapple into 4 equal-sized rings.
3. Lightly grease the grill grates with cooking spray or a small brush of olive oil to prevent sticking.
4. Place the pineapple rings onto the grill. Cook for about 6-7 minutes on each side, or until the pineapple has nice grill marks and begins to caramelize.
5. In a small bowl, mix together the honey and cinnamon until well combined.
6. Once the pineapple is grilled, immediately drizzle the honey-cinnamon mixture over the warm pineapple rings, allowing it to glaze the fruit.
7. Serve the grilled pineapple warm, as the honey drizzle continues to soak into the pineapple.
8. Enjoy this sweet, warm dessert that's not only delicious but also friendly to your cholesterol levels.

Pear and Ginger Compote

Time: 30 minutes

Serving Size: 4 servings

Prep Time: 10 minutes

Cook Time: 20 minutes

Nutrition Information Per Serving (1 serving unit):

Calories: 150, Carbohydrates: 39g, Saturated Fat: 0g, Protein: 1g, Fat: 0g, Sodium: 2mg, Potassium: 212mg, Fiber: 5g, Sugar: 28g, Vitamin C: 7mg, Calcium: 16mg, Iron: 0.3mg.

Ingredients:

- 4 ripe pears, peeled, cored, and chopped
- 1 tablespoon fresh ginger, finely grated
- 1 cinnamon stick
- Juice of 1 lemon
- 1/4 cup water
- 2 tablespoons honey (optional, for sweetness)

Directions:

1. In a medium-sized saucepan, combine the chopped pears, freshly grated ginger, and the cinnamon stick.
2. Add the juice of one lemon and water to the mixture.
3. Stir gently to combine. If you prefer a sweeter taste, add the honey to the mixture. Place the saucepan over medium heat and bring the mixture to a gentle simmer. Reduce the heat and allow it to cook for 20 minutes, stirring occasionally.
4. The compote is ready once the pears are soft and the flavors have melded together nicely.
5. Remove the cinnamon stick before serving. Serve the compote warm or allow it to cool down before refrigerating.
6. It can be enjoyed as a dessert on its own or as a topping for low-fat yogurt or oatmeal.
7. Remember to keep the serving size in mind to maintain the nutritional balance.

Chapter 10: Beverages

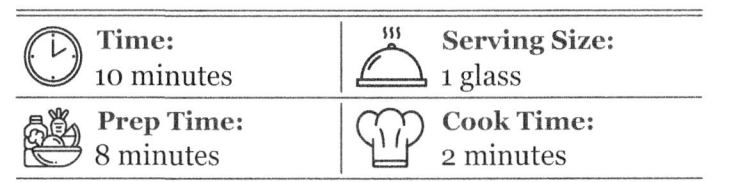

Green Tea Smoothie

Time: 10 minutes	Serving Size: 1 glass
Prep Time: 8 minutes	Cook Time: 2 minutes

Nutrition Information Per Serving (1 glass):

Calories: 150, Carbohydrates: 32g, Saturated Fat: 0.5g, Protein: 6g, Fat: 1g, Sodium: 42mg, Potassium: 670mg, Fiber: 5g, Sugar: 18g, Vitamin C: 14mg, Calcium: 200mg, Iron: 1.2mg.

Ingredients:

- 1 cup brewed green tea, cooled
- 1 ripe banana
- 1/2 cup unsweetened almond milk
- 1 cup fresh spinach leaves
- 1/2 cup frozen mixed berries
- 1 tablespoon ground flaxseed
- 1 teaspoon honey (optional)

Directions:

1. Start by brewing 1 cup of green tea and allow it to cool; this can be done ahead of time and kept in the refrigerator.
2. In a blender, combine the cooled green tea, 1 ripe banana, and 1/2 cup of unsweetened almond milk. Blend until smooth.
3. Add 1 cup of fresh spinach leaves and 1/2 cup of frozen mixed berries to the blender.
4. Include 1 tablespoon of ground flaxseed for a dose of omega-3 fatty acids.
5. If a touch of sweetness is desired, add 1 teaspoon of honey.
6. Blend all the ingredients until smooth and creamy. If the smoothie is too thick, add a little more almond milk or water to reach your preferred consistency.
7. Serve immediately and enjoy your heart-healthy Green Tea Smoothie.

Vegetable Juice Blend

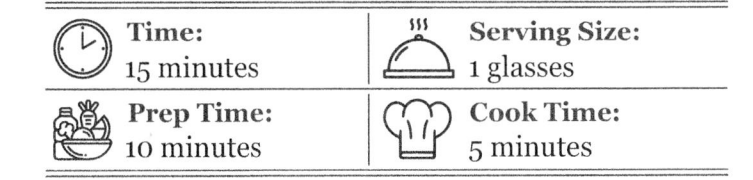

Time: 15 minutes	Serving Size: 1 glasses
Prep Time: 10 minutes	Cook Time: 5 minutes

Nutrition Information Per Serving (1 glass):

Calories: 118, Carbohydrates: 27g, Saturated Fat: 0g, Protein: 4g, Fat: 1g, Sodium: 68mg, Potassium: 897mg, Fiber: 5g, Sugar: 14g, Vitamin C: 70%, Calcium: 7%, Iron: 15%.

Ingredients:

- 2 medium carrots, peeled
- 1 small beet, peeled and quartered
- 1 celery stalk
- 1 cup of spinach leaves
- 1 green apple, cored and sliced
- 1/2 inch piece of

ginger, peeled
- 1 lemon, juiced
- 1/2 cucumber
- 1 cup of water

Directions:

1. In a high-powered blender, add 1 cup of water, 2 peeled medium carrots, 1 small quartered beet, 1 celery stalk, 1 cup of spinach leaves, 1 cored and sliced green apple, and a 1/2 inch piece of ginger.
2. Blend on high until all the vegetables are completely liquefied. If the mixture is too thick, add water in small amounts until the desired consistency is reached.
3. Take the lemon and juice it, discarding any seeds.
4. Add the lemon juice to the blended mixture.
5. Slice 1/2 a cucumber and add it to the blender. Blend again for about 1 minute or until the juice is smooth.
6. Strain the juice through a fine-mesh sieve or cheesecloth into a large pitcher to remove the pulp (optional).
7. Serve the juice immediately or store in the refrigerator in an airtight container for up to 24 hours for the best flavor and nutrient retention.
8. Before serving, stir or shake well as natural separation may occur.

Herbal Iced Tea with Lemon

Time: 30 minutes	Serving Size: 4 cups
Prep Time: 5 minutes	Cook Time: 25 minutes

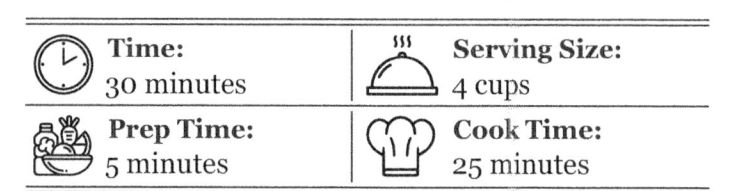

Nutrition Information Per Serving (1 cup):
Calories: 2, Carbohydrates: 0.7g, Saturated Fat: 0g, Protein: 0g, Fat: 0g, Sodium: 2mg, Potassium: 9mg, Fiber: 0g, Sugar: 0.2g, Vitamin C: 9.7mg, Calcium: 4mg, Iron: 0mg.

Ingredients:
- 4 cups of water
- 4 herbal tea bags (caffeine-free)
- Peel of 1 lemon (avoid the white pith to reduce bitterness)
- Fresh mint leaves (for garnish)
- Ice cubes
- Lemon slices (for garnish)

Directions:

1. In a medium saucepan, bring 4 cups of water to a simmer, but do not let it come to a full boil to prevent over-extraction of bitter flavors from the herbs.
2. Once the water is simmering, turn off the heat and add the 4 herbal tea bags and the peel of 1 lemon into the water.
3. Allow the tea to steep for about 5 minutes, or according to the tea package instructions. If you desire a stronger flavor, you can steep for a few minutes longer, but be cautious not to over-steep as it can become bitter.
4. After steeping, remove the tea bags and lemon peel from the saucepan and let the tea cool to room temperature for about 20 minutes.
5. Once cooled, pour the tea into a pitcher and place it in the refrigerator to chill for about 1 hour. If you're in a hurry, you can skip this step and serve immediately over ice cubes.
6. To serve, fill glasses with ice cubes, pour the chilled tea over the ice, and garnish each glass with a slice of lemon and a sprig of fresh mint.
7. Enjoy your refreshing Herbal Iced Tea with Lemon!

Almond Milk Hot Cocoa

Time: 15 minutes	Serving Size: 1 cup
Prep Time: 5 minutes	Cook Time: 10 minutes

Nutrition Information Per Serving (1 cup):

Calories: 150, Carbohydrates: 20g, Saturated Fat: 0.5g, Protein: 2g, Fat: 4g, Sodium: 95mg, Potassium: 150mg, Fiber: 3g, Sugar: 12g, Vitamin C: 0%, Calcium: 300mg, Iron: 1mg.

Ingredients:

- 2 cups unsweetened almond milk
- 2 tablespoons unsweetened cocoa powder
- 1 tablespoon maple syrup (or to taste)
- 1/4 teaspoon vanilla extract
- Pinch of sea salt

Directions:

1. In a small pot, gently heat the unsweetened almond milk over medium heat until it begins to warm.
2. Be careful not to bring it to a boil to preserve the delicate flavors.
3. Whisk in the unsweetened cocoa powder until there are no lumps and the cocoa is fully incorporated into the almond milk.
4. Stir in the maple syrup, adjusting the amount to your preference for sweetness.
5. Add a pinch of sea salt, which will help to balance the flavors and enhance the chocolatey taste.
6. Finally, stir in the vanilla extract for a hint of warmth and complexity.
7. Continue to heat the mixture for about 10 minutes, frequently stirring, until the hot cocoa is heated through to your liking.
8. Pour into a mug and enjoy your heartwarming beverage!

Berry and Spinach Smoothie

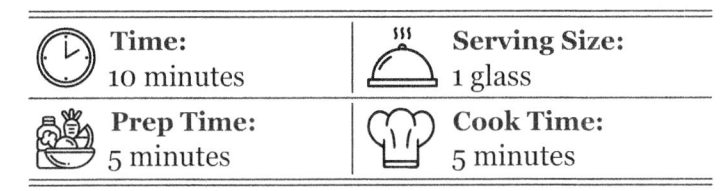

Time: 10 minutes	Serving Size: 1 glass
Prep Time: 5 minutes	Cook Time: 5 minutes

Nutrition Information Per Serving (1 glass):

Calories: 150, Carbohydrates: 22g, Saturated Fat: 0g, Protein: 5g, Fat: 1g, Sodium: 50mg, Potassium: 670mg, Fiber: 6g, Sugar: 12g, Vitamin C: 40mg, Calcium: 75mg, Iron: 2mg.

Ingredients:

- 1 cup fresh spinach leaves
- 1/2 cup frozen mixed berries (blueberries, raspberries, blackberries)
- 1/2 banana, sliced
- 1 tablespoon chia seeds
- 1 cup unsweetened almond milk
- 1/2 cup plain Greek yogurt
- 1 teaspoon honey (optional)
- Ice cubes (optional)

Directions:

1. In a blender, combine 1 cup of fresh spinach leaves and 1/2 cup of frozen mixed berries.
2. Add the 1/2 sliced banana to the blender for natural sweetness and creamy texture.
3. Sprinkle in 1 tablespoon of chia seeds for added fiber and nutrients.
4. Pour in 1 cup of unsweetened almond milk; you can add more if you prefer a thinner smoothie.
5. Add 1/2 cup of plain Greek yogurt to incorporate protein and a rich, smooth consistency.
6. For a touch of sweetness, blend in 1 teaspoon

of honey if desired.

7. Add a few ice cubes to the blender if you like your smoothie cold.

8. Blend on high speed until all the ingredients are well combined and the smoothie reaches your preferred consistency.

9. Pour the smoothie into a glass and enjoy immediately.

Tomato and Cucumber Gazpacho

Time: 15 minutes	Serving Size: 1 cup
Prep Time: 15 minutes	Cook Time: 0 minutes

Nutrition Information Per Serving (1 bowl):

Calories: 120, Carbohydrates: 18g, Saturated Fat: 0.5g, Protein: 3g, Fat: 5g, Sodium: 70mg, Potassium: 650mg, Fiber: 4g, Sugar: 10g, Vitamin C: 40%, Calcium: 4%, Iron: 8%.

Ingredients:

- 1 large cucumber, peeled and chopped
- 2 medium tomatoes, chopped
- 1/2 red onion, chopped
- 1 small bell pepper, red or yellow, seeded and chopped
- 1 garlic clove, minced
- 1 tablespoon olive oil
- 2 teaspoons balsamic vinegar
- 1/2 teaspoon mustard
- A pinch of salt (optional)
- A pinch of freshly ground black pepper
- 1/2 cup low-sodium vegetable broth
- Fresh herbs (such as basil or parsley), for garnish

Directions:

1. In a blender or food processor, combine the cucumber, tomatoes, red onion, and bell pepper.

2. Blend until the mixture reaches your desired consistency for gazpacho, either slightly chunky or smooth.

3. Add the minced garlic, olive oil, balsamic vinegar, mustard, a pinch of salt (if using), and freshly ground black pepper to the mixture.

4. Blend again to incorporate all the flavors.

5. Pour the gazpacho into a large bowl and stir in the low-sodium vegetable broth to reach a soup-like consistency.

6. Taste and adjust the seasoning if necessary.

7. Chill the gazpacho in the refrigerator for at least 1 hour before serving to allow the flavors to meld together.

8. Serve the gazpacho in cups or bowls, garnished with fresh herbs of your choice.

Coconut Water and Pineapple Juice

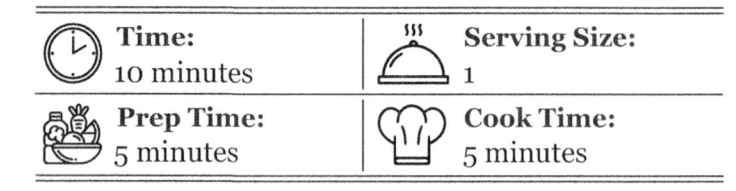

Time: 10 minutes	Serving Size: 1
Prep Time: 5 minutes	Cook Time: 5 minutes

Nutrition Information Per Serving (1 glass):

Calories: 150, Carbohydrates: 39g, Saturated Fat: 0g, Protein: 2g, Fat: 0g, Sodium: 25mg, Potassium: 600mg, Fiber: 2g, Sugar: 30g, Vitamin C: 140%, Calcium: 6%, Iron: 4%.

Ingredients:

- 1 cup fresh pineapple juice
- 1 cup coconut water
- Ice cubes (optional)
- Fresh pineapple slices for garnish
- Fresh mint leaves for garnish

Directions:

1. In a blender, combine 1 cup of fresh pineapple juice with 1 cup of coconut water.

Blend these together until well mixed.

2. If a chilled beverage is preferred, add ice cubes to the blender and pulse until the ice is crushed and the drink is cold.
3. Pour the mixture into a glass, garnish with a slice of fresh pineapple and a few mint leaves.
4. Serve immediately and enjoy your refreshing, cholesterol-friendly Coconut Water and Pineapple Juice.

Carrot and Ginger Juice

Time: 10 minutes	Serving Size: 2 glasses
Prep Time: 5 minutes	Cook Time: 5 minutes

Nutrition Information Per Serving (1 glass):

Calories: 95, Carbohydrates: 22g, Saturated Fat: 0g, Protein: 2g, Fat: 0.5g, Sodium: 70mg, Potassium: 689mg, Fiber: 5g, Sugar: 9g, Vitamin C: 20%, Calcium: 5%, Iron: 5%.

Ingredients:

- 6 large carrots, peeled
- 1-inch piece of fresh ginger, peeled
- 1 tablespoon of fresh lemon juice
- 1 cup of cold water
- Ice cubes (optional)
- Fresh mint leaves for garnish (optional)

Directions:

1. In a blender, combine the peeled carrots, fresh ginger, lemon juice, and cold water. Blend on high speed until the mixture is smooth.
2. If desired, strain the mixture through a fine mesh sieve to remove the pulp for a smoother juice.
3. Pour the juice into glasses over ice cubes if using.
4. Garnish with fresh mint leaves to add a refreshing touch.
5. Serve immediately and enjoy your heart-healthy beverage.

Beetroot and Apple Smoothie

Time: 10 minutes	Serving Size: 1 glass
Prep Time: 5 minutes	Cook Time: 5 minutes

Nutrition Information Per Serving (1 glass):

Calories: 150, Carbohydrates: 35g, Saturated Fat: 0g, Protein: 3g, Fat: 1g, Sodium: 60mg, Potassium: 600mg, Fiber: 6g, Sugar: 25g, Vitamin C: 30%, Calcium: 4%, Iron: 10%.

Ingredients:

- 1 medium beetroot, peeled and chopped
- 1 large apple, cored and chopped
- 1 cup unsweetened almond milk
- 1 tablespoon flaxseeds
- 1 teaspoon honey (optional)
- ½ teaspoon freshly grated ginger
- A pinch of ground cinnamon
- Ice cubes (optional)

Directions:

1. Begin by preparing your ingredients: peel and chop one medium beetroot and core and chop one large apple.
2. In a blender, combine the chopped beetroot and apple with one cup of unsweetened almond milk.
3. Add a tablespoon of flaxseeds for added fiber and omega-3 fatty acids.
4. If you prefer a slight sweetness, add a teaspoon of honey.
5. Include half a teaspoon of freshly grated ginger and a pinch of ground cinnamon for a

warming flavor.

6. Blend the mixture until smooth.
7. If you like your smoothie chilled, you can blend in a few ice cubes as well.
8. Once the texture is creamy and smooth, pour the smoothie into a glass and enjoy your heart-healthy beverage.

Lemon and Mint Infused Water

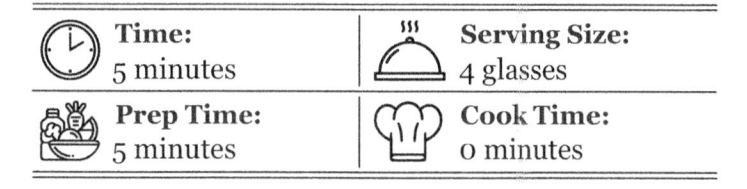

Time: 5 minutes	Serving Size: 4 glasses
Prep Time: 5 minutes	Cook Time: 0 minutes

Nutrition Information Per Serving (1 glass):

Calories: 10, Carbohydrates: 3g, Saturated Fat: 0g, Protein: 0g, Fat: 0g, Sodium: 0mg, Potassium: 49mg, Fiber: 1g, Sugar: 0g, Vitamin C: 14.6mg, Calcium: 22mg, Iron: 0.1mg.

Ingredients:

- 4 cups of filtered water
- 1 lemon, thinly sliced
- 10 fresh mint leaves

Directions:

1. Fill a large pitcher with 4 cups of filtered water.
2. Take the lemon and slice it thinly, ensuring you remove any seeds that may be present.
3. Add the lemon slices to the pitcher of water.
4. Take 10 fresh mint leaves, give them a gentle clap between your hands to release their aroma and essential oils, and then add them to the pitcher.
5. Stir the lemon slices and mint leaves with a long spoon to ensure they are evenly distributed.
6. Place the pitcher in the refrigerator to infuse for at least an hour or serve immediately over ice for a refreshing and hydrating beverage.
7. To serve, pour the infused water into glasses, making sure to include a couple of lemon slices and mint leaves in each glass for garnish and added flavor.

Pomegranate and Blueberry Spritzer

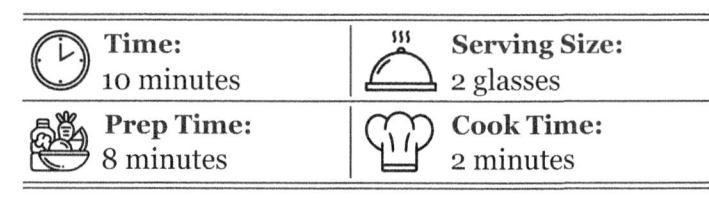

Time: 10 minutes	Serving Size: 2 glasses
Prep Time: 8 minutes	Cook Time: 2 minutes

Nutrition Information Per Serving (1 glass):

Calories: 120, Carbohydrates: 30g, Saturated Fat: 0g, Protein: 1g, Fat: 0g, Sodium: 20mg, Potassium: 250mg, Fiber: 3g, Sugar: 25g, Vitamin C: 20%, Calcium: 2%, Iron: 2%.

Ingredients:

- 1 cup fresh pomegranate juice (no added sugar)
- 1/2 cup fresh blueberries
- 2 cups sparkling water, chilled
- Ice cubes (optional)
- Fresh mint leaves for garnish (optional)

Directions:

1. Begin by preparing the pomegranate juice. If using a fresh pomegranate, cut it open, remove the arils, and use a juicer to extract the juice. You should have about 1 cup of juice.
2. Take a handful of fresh blueberries and, in a small bowl, lightly muddle them to release their juices and flavors.
3. In a pitcher, combine the muddled blueberries and pomegranate juice. Stir gently to mix.
4. Add the chilled sparkling water to the

pomegranate and blueberry mixture and stir lightly to combine. If you prefer a sweeter drink, you can add a touch of honey or agave syrup and stir well to dissolve.

5. If desired, add ice cubes to two glasses.
6. Pour the spritzer mixture evenly into the glasses, ensuring that blueberries are distributed in each glass.
7. Garnish with fresh mint leaves for a refreshing aroma and a burst of color.
8. Serve immediately and enjoy your heart-healthy Pomegranate and Blueberry Spritzer.

Chamomile and Honey Tea

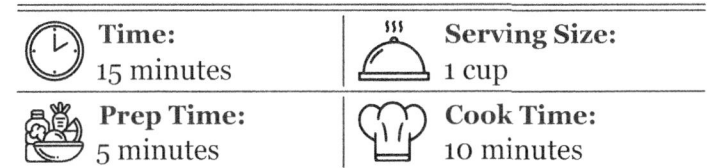

Time: 15 minutes	Serving Size: 1 cup
Prep Time: 5 minutes	Cook Time: 10 minutes

Nutrition Information Per Serving (1 cup):

Calories: 64, Carbohydrates: 17g, Saturated Fat: 0g, Protein: 0g, Fat: 0g, Sodium: 12mg, Potassium: 21mg, Fiber: 0g, Sugar: 17g, Vitamin C: 0.1mg, Calcium: 5mg, Iron: 0.12mg.

Ingredients:

- 1 chamomile tea bag
- 1 cup (240 mL) of boiling water
- 1 tablespoon of honey
- Optional: a slice of lemon for garnish

Directions:

1. Begin by boiling 1 cup (240 mL) of water.
2. Once the water reaches a rolling boil, pour it into a teapot or a heat-resistant cup.
3. Place the chamomile tea bag into the water and allow it to steep for 5 minutes.
4. This duration will ensure that the flavors and properties of the chamomile are well infused.
5. After steeping, remove the tea bag and add 1 tablespoon of honey to the infusion.
6. Stir well until the honey is completely dissolved.
7. For an added touch of flavor and vitamin C, you can garnish with a slice of lemon.
8. Serve the tea while it's warm to enjoy its soothing properties.

Turmeric and Ginger Latte

Time: 15 minutes	Serving Size: 1 cup
Prep Time: 5 minutes	Cook Time: 10 minutes

Nutrition Information Per Serving (1 cup):

Calories: 74, Carbohydrates: 9g, Saturated Fat: 0.5g, Protein: 1g, Fat: 3.5g, Sodium: 20mg, Potassium: 150mg, Fiber: 0.7g, Sugar: 7g, Vitamin C: 0.7mg, Calcium: 159mg, Iron: 0.9mg.

Ingredients:

- 1 cup unsweetened almond milk
- 1/2 teaspoon ground turmeric
- 1/4 teaspoon ground ginger
- 1 tablespoon honey, or to taste
- 1/4 teaspoon vanilla extract
- Pinch of ground black pepper (to enhance turmeric absorption)
- Cinnamon stick or ground cinnamon for garnish (optional)

Directions:

1. In a small saucepan, gently heat the unsweetened almond milk over medium heat until warm but not boiling.
2. Whisk in the ground turmeric, ground ginger, honey, and vanilla extract until fully combined.
3. Continue to heat the mixture for about 5

minutes, stirring occasionally, making sure it doesn't come to a boil.

4. Add a pinch of ground black pepper and stir into the latte.

5. Pour the latte into a mug through a fine strainer if desired.

6. Garnish with a cinnamon stick or a sprinkle of ground cinnamon for an extra hint of warmth and flavor.

7. Enjoy your heartwarming Turmeric and Ginger Latte immediately.

Chapter 11: 28-Day Meal Prep Plan

Week 1

Day 1

Breakfast: Oatmeal with Fresh Berries and Almonds

Lunch: Grilled Chicken Salad with Mixed Greens

Snack or appetizer: Carrot and Cucumber Sticks with Hummus

Dinner: Stuffed Bell Peppers with Lentils

Day 2

Breakfast: Spinach and Mushroom Egg White Omelette

Lunch: Turkey Lettuce Wraps

Snack or appetizer: Roasted Chickpeas with Paprika

Dinner: Grilled Flank Steak with Chimichurri

Day 3

Breakfast: Avocado Toast on Whole Grain Bread

Lunch: Chicken and Vegetable Stir-Fry

Snack or appetizer: Almonds and Walnuts Trail Mix

Dinner: Grilled Salmon with Lemon and Dill

Day 4

Breakfast: Greek Yogurt Parfait with Honey and Nuts

Lunch: Baked Chicken with Herbs and Lemon

Snack or appetizer: Baked Kale Chips

Dinner: Vegetarian Chili

Day 5

Breakfast: Banana Pancakes with Low-Fat Yogurt Topping

Lunch: Turkey Quinoa Meatballs

Snack or appetizer: Stuffed Bell Peppers with Quinoa

Dinner: Baked Cod with Tomato and Basil

Day 6

Breakfast: Smoothie Bowl with Chia Seeds and Kiwi

Lunch: Chicken and Broccoli Alfredo (with Whole Wheat Pasta)

Snack or appetizer: Edamame with Sea Salt

Dinner: Vegan Lentil Burgers

Day 7

Breakfast: Whole Wheat Veggie Wraps

Lunch: Turkey Chili with Beans

Snack or appetizer: Fruit Kebabs with Yogurt Dip

Dinner: Beef and Broccoli Stir-Fry

Week 2

Day 8

Breakfast: Oatmeal with Fresh Berries and Almonds

Lunch: Grilled Chicken Salad with Mixed Greens

Snack or appetizer: Carrot and Cucumber Sticks with Hummus

Dinner: Vegetarian Chili

Day 9

Breakfast: Greek Yogurt Parfait with Honey and Nuts

Lunch: Turkey Lettuce Wraps

Snack or appetizer: Roasted Chickpeas with Paprika

Dinner: Stuffed Bell Peppers with Lentils

Day 10

Breakfast: Banana Pancakes with Low-Fat Yogurt Topping

Lunch: Chicken and Vegetable Stir-Fry

Snack or appetizer: Almonds and Walnuts Trail Mix

Dinner: Grilled Salmon with Lemon and Dill

Day 11

Breakfast: Avocado Toast on Whole Grain Bread

Lunch: Baked Lemon Pepper Chicken

Snack or appetizer: Baked Kale Chips

Dinner: Beef and Broccoli Stir-Fry

Day 12

Breakfast: Smoothie Bowl with Chia Seeds and Kiwi

Lunch: Turkey Quinoa Meatballs

Snack or appetizer: Fruit Kebabs with Yogurt Dip

Dinner: Baked Cod with Tomato and Basil

Day 13

Breakfast: Whole Wheat Veggie Wraps

Lunch: Chicken Fajitas with Whole Wheat Tortillas

Snack or appetizer: Zucchini Fritters

Dinner: Sirloin Steak with Grilled Vegetables

Day 14

Breakfast: Baked Sweet Potato and Kale Hash

Lunch: Moroccan Spiced Chicken Skewers

Snack or appetizer: Caprese Salad Skewers

Dinner: Seafood Paella (with Brown Rice)

Week 3

Day 15

Breakfast: Quinoa Porridge with Cinnamon Apples

Lunch: BBQ Pulled Chicken (with Homemade Low-Sugar Sauce)

Snack or appetizer: Rice Cakes with Avocado Spread

Dinner: Vegan Lentil Burgers

Day 16

Breakfast: Low-Fat Cottage Cheese with Pineapple

Lunch: Herb Roasted Turkey Breast

Snack or appetizer: Roasted Brussel Sprouts with Balsamic Glaze

Dinner: Tuna Salad Stuffed Avocado

Day 17

Breakfast: Vegan Tofu Scramble with Tomatoes

Lunch: Lean Beef Burgers with Whole Wheat Buns

Snack or appetizer: Sweet Potato Wedges with Low-Fat Greek Yogurt Dip

Dinner: Zucchini Lasagna (with Tofu Ricotta)

Day 18

Breakfast: Overnight Chia Seed Pudding

Lunch: Baked Chicken with Herbs and Lemon

Snack or appetizer: Baked Apple Chips

Dinner: Grilled Flank Steak with Chimichurri

Day 19

Breakfast: Whole Grain Blueberry Muffins

Lunch: Chicken Vegetable Soup

Snack or appetizer: Edamame with Sea Salt

Dinner: Stir-Fried Quinoa with Veggies

Day 20

Breakfast: Spinach and Mushroom Egg White Omelette

Lunch: Beef Stew with Root Vegetables

Snack or appetizer: Stuffed Bell Peppers with Quinoa

Dinner: Stir-Fry with Mixed Vegetables

Day 21

Breakfast: Banana Bread with Almond Flour

Lunch: Salmon Patties with Whole Wheat Breadcrumbs

Snack or appetizer: Roasted Brussel Sprouts with Balsamic Glaze

Dinner: Spaghetti Squash with Marinara Sauce

Week 4

Day 22

Breakfast: Quinoa Porridge with Cinnamon Apples

Lunch: Baked Lemon Pepper Chicken

Snack or appetizer: Carrot and Cucumber Sticks with Hummus

Dinner: Vegetable Curry with Brown Rice

Day 23

Breakfast: Greek Yogurt Parfait with Honey and Nuts

Lunch: Turkey Chili with Beans

Snack or appetizer: Almonds and Walnuts Trail Mix

Dinner: Baked Tilapia with Roasted Vegetables

Day 24

Breakfast: Oatmeal with Fresh Berries and Almonds

Lunch: Chicken and Broccoli Alfredo (with Whole Wheat Pasta)

Snack or appetizer: Zucchini Fritters

Dinner: Vegan Shepherd's Pie

Day 25

Breakfast: Smoothie Bowl with Chia Seeds and Kiwi

Lunch: Beef Lettuce Wraps

Snack or appetizer: Edamame with Sea Salt

Dinner: Stuffed Bell Peppers with Quinoa

Day 26

Breakfast: Baked Sweet Potato and Kale Hash

Lunch: Beef Fajitas with Whole Wheat Tortillas

Snack or appetizer: Roasted Chickpeas with Paprika

Dinner: Mushroom Stroganoff

Day 27

Breakfast: Vegan Tofu Scramble with Tomatoes

Lunch: Grilled Scallops with Lemon Butter Sauce

Snack or appetizer: Fruit Kebabs with Yogurt Dip

Dinner: Roasted Cauliflower Tacos

Day 28

Breakfast: Whole Grain Blueberry Muffins

Lunch: Beef and Barley Soup

Snack or appetizer: Caprese Salad Skewers

Dinner: Vegan Paella with Bell Peppers and Peas

Free Gift

Thank you! Discover your gift inside! Dive into a rich assortment of DASH Diet for Beginners recipes for added inspiration. Gift it or share the PDF effortlessly with friends and family via a single click on WhatsApp or other social platforms. Bon appétit!

Conclusion outline

Embarking on a journey to lower your cholesterol can be a transformative experience for your health and well-being. Throughout the pages of this «Low Cholesterol Cookbook Diet for Beginners,» we've ventured into a culinary realm that not only satisfies your palate but also serves your heart. Let's recap our adventure.

The recipes presented in this book are meticulously designed to be low in saturated fat, trans fats, and cholesterol, which are pivotal for managing and improving your heart health. We've discussed the importance of incorporating soluble fiber and plant sterols into your diet, which have been shown to naturally lower cholesterol levels. From fiber-rich breakfasts to omega-3-packed dinners, every recipe was crafted to deliver maximum flavor while supporting your cardiovascular system.

We haven't overlooked snacks and desserts, because a balanced diet allows for occasional indulgences—crafted with heart health in mind. This cookbook is more than a collection of recipes; it's an educational tool that empowers you to make conscious food choices every day. Adherence to a low-cholesterol diet involves understanding the ingredients in your food, reading labels with a discerning eye, and maintaining awareness of serving sizes.

Remember that this dietary approach is adaptable. Feel free to substitute ingredients that you prefer or those that better fit your nutritional goals, provided they align with a heart-healthy profile. It's not solely about avoiding certain foods; it's about embracing a diverse array of nutritious options that contribute to your heart's vitality.

As you continue on this path, approach it one meal at a time. Master one recipe, enjoy it, and then introduce another. Soon, you'll have an extensive collection of low-cholesterol dishes to choose from. Should you need guidance, don't hesitate to consult a nutritionist or your healthcare provider to tailor these recipes to your individual health needs. They are your partners in your journey towards a heart-healthy lifestyle.

In conclusion, this cookbook marks the beginning of your commitment to a heart-healthy life. It's about discovering the joy of cooking and the peace of mind that comes with knowing you're nourishing your body in the best way possible. So, grab your whisk, preheat your oven, and prepare to embark on a culinary journey. Your heart—and your tastebuds—will be grateful.

References

Turner, S. (2023). «Heart-Healthy Haven: A Low Cholesterol Culinary Adventure.» NutriWell Publications.

https://www.nutriwellpub.com/hhhlcc

Cruz, B. (2023). «Savory Seafood Delights: A Low Cholesterol Cookbook.» WholesomeReads.

https://www.wholesomereads.com/ssd-lcc

Anderson, N. (2023). «Cholesterol Chronicles: A Beginner's Guide to Heart-Healthy Living.» HealthFusion Blog.

https://www.healthfusionblog.com/ccbhhl

Manning, E. (2022). «Low Cholesterol Lifestyle: Exploring the Benefits.» CulinaryPerspectives Journal, 15(4), 203-217. https://www.culinaryperspectivesjournal.com/lcl-eb

Wong, I. (2023). «Flavorful Foundations: A Low Cholesterol Cookbook for Beginners.» GourmetGuidance

https://www.gourmetguidance.com/fflccfb

Taylor, A. (2023). «Heartful Eats: A Journey into Low Cholesterol Delicacies.» CookBookVista.

https://www.cookbookvista.com/heartful-eats

Perez, C. (2022). «Balancing Act: The Interplay of Diet and Cholesterol.» HealthyLiving Journal, 12(3), 112-126

https://www.healthylivingjournal.com/ba-idc

Roberts, O. (2023). «Low Cholesterol Gourmet: A Culinary Exploration.» EpicureanElegance.

https://www.epicureanelegance.com/lcg-ce

Barnes, M. (2023). «Fresh Flavors for a Healthy Heart: Low Cholesterol Recipes.» CulinaryCrafts Blog.

https://www.culinarycraftsblog.com/ffhh-lcr

Gomez, A. (2023). «Cooking for Cardiovascular Health: A Low Cholesterol Primer.» HeartfulHarmony.

https://www.heartfulharmony.com/cch-lcp

Appendix 1: Measurement Conversion Chart

U.S. System	Metric
1 inch	2.54 centimeters
1 fluid ounce	29.57 milliliters
1 pint (16 ounces)	473.18 milliliters, 2 cups
1 quart (32 ounces)	1 liter, 4 cups
1 gallon (128 ounces)	4 liters, 16 cups
1 pound (16 ounces)	437.5 grams (0.4536 kilogram), 473.18 milliliters
1 ounces	2 tablespoons, 28 grams
1 cup (8 ounces)	237 milliliters
1 teaspoon	5 milliliters
1 tablespoon	15 milliliters (3 teaspoons)
Fahrenheit (subtract 32 and divide by 1.8 to get Celsius)	Centigrade (multiply by 1.8 and add 32 to get Fahrenheit)

Appendix 2: Index Recipes

A

Almonds

Oatmeal with Fresh Berries and Almonds - 13

Greek Yogurt Parfait with Honey and Nuts - 15

Almonds and Walnuts Trail Mix - 22

Avocado

Avocado Toast on Whole Grain Bread - 14

Rice Cakes with Avocado Spread - 26

B

Banana

Banana Pancakes with Low-Fat Yogurt Topping - 15

Beans

Turkey Chili with Beans - 33

Beef

Lean Beef Burgers with Whole Wheat Buns - 49

Beef and Broccoli Stir-Fry - 48

Beef and Mushroom Skewers - 52

Beets

Roasted Beet and Goat Cheese Salad - 66

Berries

Smoothie Bowl with Chia Seeds and Kiwi - 16

Low-Fat Berry Yogurt Parfait - 75

Blueberries

Whole Grain Blueberry Muffins - 20

Peach and Blueberry Crumble - 77

Broccoli

Chicken and Broccoli Alfredo (with Whole Wheat Pasta) - 32

Broccoli and Apple Salad with Walnuts - 71

C

Carrots

Carrot and Cucumber Sticks with Hummus - 21

Carrot Cake with Low-Fat Cream Cheese Frosting - 78

Cauliflower

Cauliflower Rice Pilaf - 70

Roasted Cauliflower Tacos - 46

Chickpeas

Roasted Chickpeas with Paprika - 21

Vegan Shepherd's Pie - 43

Chicken

Grilled Chicken Salad with Mixed Greens - 29

Baked Chicken with Herbs and Lemon - 31

Chicken Fajitas with Whole Wheat Tortillas - 35

Chia Seeds

Overnight Chia Seed Pudding - 19

Smoothie Bowl with Chia Seeds and Kiwi - 16

Chocolate

Vegan Chocolate Mousse - 79

Cinnamon

Quinoa Porridge with Cinnamon Apples - 18

Baked Apples with Cinnamon - 75

Cod

Baked Cod with Tomato and Basil - 57

Corn

Sweet Corn and Black Bean Salad - 68

Couscous

Couscous with Roasted Veggies - 68

D

Dark Chocolate

Dark Chocolate-Dipped Strawberries - **76**

E

Eggplant

Eggplant Parmesan (Vegan Version) - **43**

Eggs

Spinach and Mushroom Egg White Omelette - **13**

F

Fish

Fish Tacos with Cabbage Slaw - **60**

Flank Steak

Grilled Flank Steak with Chimichurri - **48**

G

Garlic

Mussels in White Wine and Garlic Sauce - **61**

Greek Yogurt

Sweet Potato Wedges with Low-Fat Greek Yogurt Dip - **27**

Green Beans

Green Beans Almondine - **74**

H

Honey

Greek Yogurt Parfait with Honey and Nuts - **15**

K

Kale

Baked Sweet Potato and Kale Hash - **17**

Kale and Quinoa Salad with Lemon Vinaigrette - **66**

Kiwi

Smoothie Bowl with Chia Seeds and Kiwi - **16**

L

Lemon

Grilled Salmon with Lemon and Dill - **57**

Lentils

Stuffed Bell Peppers with Lentils - **38**

M

Mushrooms

Spinach and Mushroom Egg White Omelette - **13**

N

Nuts

Greek Yogurt Parfait with Honey and Nuts - **15**

O

Oats

Lean Meatloaf with Oats - **54**

P

Pasta

Chicken and Broccoli Alfredo (with Whole Wheat Pasta) - **32**

Peppers

Stuffed Bell Peppers with Quinoa - **23**

Pineapple

Low-Fat Cottage Cheese with Pineapple - **18**

Potatoes

Baked Sweet Potato and Kale Hash - **17**

Q

Quinoa

Whole Wheat Veggie Wraps - **16**

Quinoa Porridge with Cinnamon Apples - **18**

R

Rice

Vegetable Curry with Brown Rice - **40**

S

Salmon

Grilled Salmon with Lemon and Dill - 57

Spinach

Spinach and Strawberry Salad - 72

Sweet Potatoes

Baked Sweet Potato and Kale Hash - 17

T

Tomatoes

Vegan Tofu Scramble with Tomatoes - 19

Tofu

Vegan Tofu Scramble with Tomatoes - 19

Turkey

Turkey Lettuce Wraps - 29

W

Walnuts

Almonds and Walnuts Trail Mix - 22

Wheat

Turkey Lettuce Wraps - 29

Whole Wheat Veggie Wraps - 16

Y

Yogurt

Greek Yogurt Parfait with Honey and Nuts - 15

Z

Zucchini

Zucchini Fritters - 24

Zucchini Lasagna (with Tofu Ricotta) - 41

Notes

Printed in Great Britain
by Amazon